Getting Financing
& Developing Land

by Michael C. Thomsett

Craftsman Book Company
6058 Corte del Cedro / P.O. Box 6500 / Carlsbad, CA 92018

Library of Congress Cataloging-in-Publication Data

Thomsett, Michael C.
    Getting financing & developing land / by Michael C. Thomsett.
      p. cm.
    Includes index.
    ISBN 1-57218-089-7
    1. Real estate development. 2. Real estate development--Finance. 3.
Real estate investment.   I. Title: Getting financing and developing
land.   II. Title.
  HD1390.T49 2000
  333.73'15'068--dc21

                           00-040470

Contents

Chapter 1

Getting Started

Anyone who embarks on a big undertaking without proper preparation is inviting disaster. This advice applies equally to generals at war, to students in school, and to business owners about to finance raw land development for the first time.

You may find books of advice about how to get money for your business, with all kinds of takes on how to go about it. Unfortunately, most of them are pretty theoretical. When it comes time for you to sit across a desk from a loan officer or venture capital investor, you need to be armed with hard information — facts and statistics. You don't want so many that they overwhelm the other person, but enough to demonstrate that you know what you're talking about. This book is designed to help you prepare for the big step, by showing you how to:

▎ Take an idea and express it in terms of specific goals.

▎ Identify the steps you need to get there.

▎ Present these ideas in the dollars and cents that bank people like to see.

Just as you need a blueprint and tools to build a house, you also need plans and tools to get the money you need to develop a project. It isn't enough to explain how interested you are in doing that project; you need to show the lender or investor how their risks are going to be managed carefully and methodically. In this book, you'll find those useful tools, including checklists, sample forms, and examples you can use to prove that your ideas make financial sense. That's the entire purpose and focus of this book.

The best and most obvious advice when you start any project is always this: "Begin at the beginning." When you're looking for financing for land development, the beginning means *defining exactly what you want*. That means answering these three questions:

1. How much do you need?

2. How will you use it?

3. How can you get it?

This book shows you how to answer those questions so you can get the money you need. Along the way, you'll learn how to:

▌ Study your operation and look for routines and procedures you'll have to change so you can manage the new demands that more complicated projects will bring.

▌ Examine the local land market, economic situation, and political climate to discover the "rules" of the development game in your community.

▌ Make informed decisions about the best and most profitable type of development for your locality and talents.

▌ Assemble and present a convincing appeal to your lender for the cash you need.

Lenders won't take chances just out of respect for your eagerness.

You're going to ask an institution or person for money you need because they have that money to loan. But they didn't get the money, or control of it, by being foolish. They're going to ask tough questions designed to find out if they're going to get their money back, and how much profit they're going to get. They're not going to take chances just out of respect for your eagerness.

So before you go looking for the money, you need to answer for yourself the questions a lender or investor will ask. There's little sense in starting up a venture before you've thoroughly explored its pitfalls and possibilities. Consider these points:

▌ Can you find suitable land?

▌ How is the land zoned?

▌ Can you get the zoning changed if you have to?

▌ Is there a demand for your project?

▌ Will your plan make money?

▌ Will the cash flow work out?

▌ What's the political climate?

▌ Are you experienced and qualified for this project?

Your answers to these questions will determine whether land development is right for you.

The Importance of Land Investment

Those who own or control the land determine how and where growth occurs.

Land — its purchase and development — is an essential element of progress. Those who own or control the land determine how and where growth occurs. Naturally, other factors, including local politics, the current state of the economy in your region, and the willingness of lenders to work with potential developers, have an effect. But the essential truth remains: Ownership and use of land is the engine of growth. As a buyer and developer of land, that makes you the engineer.

Here are some statistics that make the case for successful land development in today's economy:

▌ Census reports estimate that population growth between 1995 and 2010 will be 36.2 percent. That's about 100 million more people and 30 to 50 million more households. And all those people will need homes and jobs. The largest increase will be in the age group between 40 and 64, as today's population ages.

▌ The aging of the population is good news for housing, commercial and industrial construction, as well as for high-end industrial properties. People in the 40-64 age group earn the most money and are the most stable in both their personal and career lives. Most families in this bracket want to own homes, can afford relatively expensive ones, and may even want a second or third home as well.

▌ New home sales for the 1990s were over 6 million, near the record set in the 1970s. During the first decade of the new millennium, the second-generation baby-boomers will get into the market, and records will probably continue to be broken.

▌ More than eight out of every 10 homes built in the United States are built by "small" builders (those having fewer than 25 employees).

Statistics also show that today's market is favorable for contractors who want to borrow money. When we talk about markets, we usually mean how many buyers there are for what we sell. But here I'm talking about the *capital market* — whether there's enough money available for you and others who want to borrow to invest in and develop land. Many sources predict that this decade will see a boom in new development. A primary cause of that boom will be the simple fact that money is available.

Planning for Land Investment

Since you're reading this book, you're already thinking about how to make money by buying and developing land. You may want to buy land and apply for a rezone, then lease, sell or develop it. Maybe you prefer a specific type of commercial or industrial development.

Developers tend to be land investors first, and builders second.

Sometimes a client will come to you with an empty lot and ask for a custom home. But that isn't how developers work — that's custom contracting. Developers tend to be land investors first, and builders second. Contractor-developers make more profit on the land than on the improvements.

Many contractors start out small. They buy a single lot and build a spec house. If all goes well, they sell it and use the profit to finance a larger, more expensive home. Perhaps you're ready to take on two or more projects at once, or move up to tract development or part of a planned community.

For all these scenarios, you'll have to create a *project plan* for a project that you can build to make a profit. Owning land isn't the end result. But it is a necessary part of the plan. And in the best of circumstances, the land will appreciate while you own it. There are a number of features that contribute to increases in land value, including improvements, more valuable use of the land, potential value created by land use changes, and the emerging path of progress which brings development pressure.

That path of progress (the direction in which growth occurs) depends on a variety of conditions:

▌ Increased employment and economic growth produce more demand for buildings of all kinds.

▌ Local governments may create progressive land use policies because they want to attract an industrial employment base.

▌ Development of transportation corridors bring tourist and travel-related activity.

▌ Other local attractions lead to changes in population, employment, and land use.

Owning the land yourself increases your profit potential. But to own land, you probably need to borrow money — and that means paying back the loan. You'll have to make those periodic loan payments on schedule *without fail*. That means your cash flow must be healthy enough so you can make regular monthly payments while you continue to pay your other bills. When you buy land for development, it won't pay for itself until it's improved. It's impossible to find a use for raw land that will cover its investment cost — other than development.

Lay a firm foundation by preparing yourself and your business for the changes that growth and expansion will bring.

You must prepare a realistic business plan and budget to offset that problem. Can you survive several months of negative cash flow while you build your project? If your project requires rezoning, you can expect a significant delay before construction starts. That will increase the time lag before profits begin to roll in.

And there's another possibility to consider. You could end up owning that land even longer than the time it takes to develop it. Many novice developers (and even some experienced ones) end up renting out a finished project when a falling market makes it impossible to sell the development at the predicted profit.

That's why you have to do your homework and lay a firm foundation by preparing yourself and your business for the changes that growth and expansion will bring. Only then can you successfully build a project that will fulfill your goals and expectations, and that will *make money*.

Speculation vs. Investment

Speculation: Assumption of unusual business risk in hopes of obtaining commensurate gain.

What's the difference between the two? The dictionary defines speculation like this: *assumption of unusual business risk in hopes of obtaining commensurate gain*. In other words, speculation is an unusually risky investment. As a contractor looking for financing to buy raw land, you could be either an investor or a speculator, or combine the characteristics of both. It all depends on the level of risk.

When you listen to the political rhetoric about land use, it can sound like all land purchasers are either angels or devils. Angels are investors who buy land to improve it for the good of the community. Investors treat their land as a personal asset to make sure that values remain high over the long term. And devils, of course, are short-term speculators who just want to make a quick buck. Speculators buy and sell land only to drive up prices and take advantage of the local folks.

Neither of these definitions is necessarily true — nothing's that black and white. But when you invest in land, sooner or later you'll run into the politics of development, where labels are used to divide the good guys from the bad guys.

You want to be one of the good guys. So when you search for financing to develop land, you need to present yourself as a responsible developer whose project will benefit rather than harm the community. No lender will be anxious to advance you money unless you can convince them of three things:

1. There's proper zoning in place (or you have a reasonable promise of getting it).

2. Your project has passed environmental review.

3. There's no strong opposition from neighborhood groups.

Before you can get the money you'll need, you have to convince the investor that local groups and politicians favor your project because they believe the community benefits outweigh any real or perceived negative consequences. They must also believe that you'll invest much of your time and a lot of your own money in the development project.

Remember that even if today's demand for your project is strong, it may weaken before you get the project finished. If your project will take two years to complete, you need to start exactly two years before the market hits peak demand for your type of project. Good luck in predicting that! The "sure thing" in real estate is rare. But you also expose yourself to risk in a number of other ways:

▌ Can you develop the management skills necessary to handle the transition from contractor to land developer?

▌ Can you find land that's priced so you can make money?

▌ Can you get the financing required to complete the project?

▌ Can you finish the job on schedule?

▌ Can you maintain a healthy cash flow during development?

We'll address the last four issues (and more) in later chapters, but for now let's consider the first one.

Prepare for Your Company's Growth

It isn't enough to just know where you want your business to go. You have to know how to get it there. Growth itself isn't hard. But keeping it on track takes special skill and attention. You have to keep one eye on the big picture while you watch the smallest details with the other.

Details have a tendency to take over. The expression, "The devil's in the details" is never more true than when it applies to running a growing business. Everything from interviewing, hiring and training a new supervisor to making sure you can rely on your office manager to keep paper clips on hand distracts your attention from the big picture — if you let it.

The Nature of Growth

If you control overhead as part of business planning, you stand a better-than-average chance of succeeding in your expansion.

The nature of growth is to dominate. If you take no action at all, it's still more likely that your company will grow than that it won't. That's because of another rule: The nature of overhead is to increase. If you've been a contractor for any time, you know this. And as your overhead increases, you're under pressure to take on more business (even if you don't want to) just to cover higher administrative expenses and continue to make a profit. But there's a better approach. Get expenses under control and keep them there.

Controlling expenses isn't just an accounting exercise. If you plan to move into new lines of business, to develop raw land by using other people's money as part of your financing plan, overhead is your "soft underbelly." If you fail to control overhead, you're at great risk. However, if you think of the control mechanisms as part of the business planning and development process, you stand a better-than-average chance of succeeding in your business expansion.

Not all aspects of growth are positive. You'll encounter many pitfalls while your company is growing. For example, growth often places personal demands on you that you didn't expect. You have to work longer hours, often for less income than you would receive as an employee — and *all* the problems are yours.

Business owners often pursue growth for its own sake, believing that growth is not only good, but necessary. You may have heard that if your business doesn't grow, it will stagnate and die. That simply isn't true. The truth is, *you* need to decide how large an operation you want, how much risk you can tolerate, and how much time you're willing to spend running the business.

But once you decide to expand your business, you need to control your rate of expansion. That means you have to put on the brakes if your company's growth happens too fast and gets out of control. You might ask, "What's wrong with fast growth?" To answer that, let's look at some of the problems associated with growth.

When you decide to expand into land development, you may be concerned about whether you'll have enough new business to sustain the growth. But that isn't the problem. The business is out there. Instead, the health of your business depends on deciding which activities to encourage and which ones to avoid.

The secret is to stay focused. Don't become so involved in a scattered collection of activities that you lose touch with what you really want — to purchase and develop raw land in a way that will return the most profit.

When is the right time to grow? The best time is when the current economy, money supply, the market and your competitive position are all favorable. If they're not, you're better off waiting until the situation changes for the better. But if you think now is the time to take the leap, consider the *expansion challenge*.

The Expansion Challenge

Expansion isn't limited to a single direction, such as upgrading equipment, producing new products or entering new markets. Expansion often occurs in several ways at the same time. We'll look at four types of expansion: volume, people, geography and competition.

Volume

Volume, People, Geography, Competition

This is the most obvious — and easiest-to-understand — type of expansion. But it involves more than just higher gross income dollars. You have to watch the rest of your profit-and-loss picture, too. If your direct costs rise to a higher percentage of sales than they were before, then you can count on one thing: lower profits.

You also need to control overhead costs so their rate of increase is far less than the increase in volume, direct costs, and gross profit. While overhead expenses invariably increase with volume expansion, there has to be a limit.

Remember that it's easier to control overhead through diligent planning and monitoring than it is to cut back once expenses have raced out of control. Controlling your overhead is the real key to higher profits after expansion.

Look at the two simplified profit summaries in Figure 1-1. In Summary 1, overhead expenses are controlled well in an environment of increased sales. Net profits increase to 22.3 percent of sales. But in the second year, in Summary 2, the same volume is accompanied by significantly higher overhead expense. The outcome is a 9.8 percent net — virtually no change from the lower volume period.

In this case, increased volume is really no more profitable. Summary 2 shows how you could expose yourself to greater risk and work harder, only to realize no real improvement in your company's operations. This is the essence of profitability — you can't just look at the numbers.

Controlling expenses is where you have the best chance of increasing your return on investment (profit divided by the amount you invested). You can't do much to reduce merchandise and labor costs. But by holding down overhead, you can significantly improve your profit when volume grows.

Overhead isn't the only thing you'll have to watch. If you plan to continue your current activities while you're managing your expansion, beware of one common pitfall. You may have a tendency to sell more on credit as your business grows. *Don't do it.* Combining higher overhead and expenses with higher accounts receivable and a slower collection cycle can be deadly. You have to plan carefully to keep your cash flow in line. Otherwise it's too easy to let your overall financial health suffer while your time and attention are focused on new operations.

More volume usually means you'll need more equipment. When you spend money for equipment, you have two choices: pay cash or borrow money. If you finance the purchase, that means interest expense and monthly payments. Before you take that step, you need to be sure that the money you need will be available from operations. Will the equipment generate enough income to cover payments? Will income begin immediately? The payments will! And is that income going to be regular or seasonal?

Equipment only generates income to the degree that it reduces labor costs. For example, a new piece of equipment may let two workers do as much as four. This cuts labor costs in half. So you can easily measure equipment productivity by comparing operating costs for current equipment against those for new and improved equipment, then balancing that against reduced labor costs.

*Equipment:
Lease or Buy?*

The answer to the question of whether to lease or buy equipment depends on current need and future plans. If you expect to use a piece of equipment over many years, it makes sense to buy it. Leasing is expensive because you're paying for time as well as equipment in exchange for a smaller

Summary 1: Expansion with Controlled Overhead		
	Year A	Year B
Sales	$518,500	$753,400
Less: Cost of Sales	264,100	377,800
Gross Profit	$254,400	$375,600
Less: General Expenses	204,600	207,500
Net Profit	$49,800	168,100
Profit (percent of sales)	9.6	22.3
Summary 2: Expansion with Excessive Overhead		
	Year A	Year B
Sales	$518,500	$753,400
Less: Cost of Sales	264,100	377,800
Gross Profit	$254,400	$375,600
Less: General Expenses	204,600	302,100
Net Profit	$49,800	$73,500
Profit (percent of sales)	9.6	9.8

Figure 1-1 Profit summaries

investment up-front. But if the equipment is something you won't need beyond the short term, a one- to three-year lease may make more sense.

When you take on larger projects, you may be forced to stockpile materials. Perhaps you won't be able to find materials in the volume you need on a dependable schedule, so you'll need to order more at one time. That usually gives you the benefit of a discount. But there's a downside. You have to pay for the inventory, you have to find a secure place to store it, and you have to insure it.

People

To support an increase in volume, you usually hire and train more people. You'll need more supervisors, office and accounting help and consultants (estimators, engineers). This means more expense. As your staff increases, you'll need more office space as well as temporary buildings at the development site. It also presents the potential for conflicts between you and your new staff about operating methods. You'll need better internal organization and scheduling to keep your trade workers busy every day.

Geography

Remote site disadvantages

All communities are limited in terms of how much construction volume they can support. Your competitors will always take their share of the local market. So when you grow, you may have to branch out to neighboring communities.

If yours has been a small company where you've supervised the job sites yourself, you may find that quality declines and work goes more slowly when you're not always physically present on the job.

Some of the disadvantages of working at a remote site are obvious:

- Higher cost to operate vehicles — fuel plus wear and tear

- Travel-time costs for employees

- Delivery charges for supplies and materials may increase

- You may have to use new, more expensive, or unfamiliar sources for services, materials and equipment

You can estimate pretty accurately what those will cost. But there are other risks that can be more expensive and harder to judge. Your presence on the job may diminish as administrative tasks take more of your time. That may translate to lower productivity by your crews, less efficient field supervision, and poorer workmanship.

It doesn't matter how diligent and trustworthy your site managers are. The fact remains that remote projects are rarely as efficient, profitable, or produced at the same level of quality as those you oversee regularly and personally. And this deterioration in operations (and profits) can become worse the farther your operation is from your home base.

Be sure to take these things into account when you consider the location for your development activities.

Competition

This is a two-edged sword. When you move into a new area or adopt new lines of business, you're confronted with a new set of competitors. These may be larger, more experienced and better financed than you are. Their proven track record might put you at a disadvantage when you approach lenders.

You may also find that businesses who didn't see you as a competitor before (when you were smaller), will now. They'll probably step up their own marketing efforts to "keep you in your place."

The best way to mitigate these challenges to expansion is to be very thorough when you prepare your market study. You'll need this document when you're ready to face a lender, and it will help you now to crystallize your plans for expansion. We'll discuss this in detail in the next chapter.

The Financing You Need

But let's return to the questions at the beginning of this chapter.

How Much Do You Need?

The size and scope of your development plan is your responsibility, not your lender's.

Unless you have a *lot* of ready cash available, financing is essential for any sizable expansion. You'll need money for the obvious things like land acquisition, surveys, reviews, permits, materials, consultants and labor — and don't forget related working cash for overhead, equipment and facilities, not to mention your own living expenses.

The amount of money you need to raise is related directly to the cost of the development. As obvious as that statement is, many people seem to forget it when they apply for a loan. Some people begin their quest for financing with the question, "How much will the lender let me have?" That's the wrong question, because it lets the lender dictate the size and scope of your development plan. That's your responsibility, not the lender's.

How Will You Use It?

When you approach a lender or investor, your task will be to show how you plan to use borrowed funds to develop your project. The size and scope of the project have to make sense. If you can demonstrate that your development has a market and is likely to be profitable, then the lender's risks are small, and so are your own.

How Can You Get It?

Think about this early in your expansion-planning stage. You might consider venture capital or taking in a partner. You may need to combine financing from many different sources to get what you want. For example, you may work with a mortgage broker to locate long-term financing for land acquisition and development, and with a commercial bank for a series of short-term working capital loans — the ones you'll need to pay the day-to-day bills.

In the early stages of development, you'll need a source for short-term financing through loans or a line of credit. It doesn't really matter how long your development project will take. You'll need flexible financing to help you during the time when expenses are high, and the income stream hasn't started flowing.

Find the Answers

Finding the answers to those three questions is the subject of the rest of this book. First, you'll learn how to approach the political aspects of land development, determine the extent of the available land inventory in your region, and analyze your market for potential buyers.

Then, based on that analysis, you'll learn how to zero in on your best development option and locate an appropriate site.

Finally, we'll cover the details of developing your project's business plan, finding the right sources for financing, presenting your plan to potential lenders or investors, dealing with objections to your plan, and managing your expansion successfully. Let's get started!

Chapter 2

The Markets

There's a lot more to the developer's market than simply finding buyers for what you have to sell. You need to start with an in-depth look at the market before you settle on the best way to make money in land development.

To gain your prospective lender's or investor's confidence, show them that your decisions and requirements are based on *reality*, not on unfounded assumptions or vague ideas. Let them know how thoroughly and accurately you've analyzed the political influences and market conditions and they'll look more favorably on your appeal for financing.

The Political Market

Your local elected officials and planning departments must be willing to endorse your plans before you can succeed as a land developer. But that's not the end of the story. Even when current zoning allows the kind of development you want to do, you may run into resistance from anti-growth groups. If you need to apply for a zoning change, conditional use permit or other variance, that resistance can be troublesome, to say the least.

In many places there's an ongoing conflict, with zealous growth-limiting advocates facing equally dedicated property rights defenders, contractors, and building industry associations. It requires persistence, time, and money to develop land when local government — or the local populace — is hostile to your plans.

Lenders don't like uncertainty, and the no-growth groups' greatest skill is creating uncertainty.

If that's the case in your area, you have an uphill battle ahead of you. In some cases, anti-growth planners can delay and block permits, or place stringent requirements on you that make it difficult (or even impossible) to proceed.

No-growth proponents, by fighting your plan in public meetings and in the press, can create uncertainty. Lenders don't like uncertainty. If the lender thinks political opposition could kill your project, that may kill your chance of a loan.

Why Do Some Governments Resist Growth?

Here are some reasons developers face this problem:

▌ Some politicians get elected simply because they promise to keep things just the way they are. They won't let anything change. They and their supporters believe that all growth is bad, and now that they have *their* piece of the pie, they don't want any more people getting a share.

▌ A second factor is purely political. Even when elected officials are pro-business and want a strong economy, a very vocal, well-organized opposition can sway votes on development projects, perhaps with the threat of opposing those officials at election time. You can't assume that even pro-growth politicians will vote for your plan.

▌ In some places, state laws restrict the ways that local governments plan for growth. The state government may even punish local jurisdictions for not following the state's planning guidelines. In these cases, local elected officials must tread the line between trying to represent those who elected them on the one hand, and complying with state law on the other. The developer, of course, is caught in the middle.

NIMBYs and BANANAs

Certainly, some local groups have correctly protected communities from exploitation by unscrupulous developers. But it's the NIMBY (Not In My Back Yard) and the BANANA (Build Absolutely Nothing Anywhere Not Anytime) groups who will cause you the most grief.

Under the banner of "quality of life," and with protecting the environment as a major tool in their arsenal, they often oppose any kind of growth, just for the sake of it. They're the ones who are most vocal at city hall and planning department hearings. One favorite quote I heard from a NIMBY during public testimony was, "I'm *not* a NIMBY. I just don't want this development anywhere near me."

If you're lucky, your city officials recognize the value of promoting growth, attracting family-wage jobs, and drawing people to your community. In such an atmosphere, everyone works together. Lenders look for opportunities to invest money. Developers and contractors thrive in a robust development market. Local politicians go out of their way to make things happen, and enjoy taking credit for the vigorous economy.

In these cases, NIMBY groups lose their energy, recognizing that their attempts to gain power over growth decisions are futile. But that isn't always the case.

You and Local Politics

Some developers sadly discover that they face organized opposition only after they take their plan to city hall to apply for zoning changes or permits. By then, they may have already bought land and invested money in a preliminary environmental review, land and soils studies, and engineering plans. You can avoid this misfortune and save a lot of time and money by testing the local political waters before you make the investment.

Attend public meetings.
Meet local political leaders.
Talk to your competitors.
Develop a political strategy.

You learn a lot about people and their stated and real beliefs and attitudes toward growth by watching them in action. You can't just read the paper, listen to the radio or watch the local TV news, because those sources might give you a biased picture of what's really going on.

You need to:

▌ Subscribe to newsletters published by your local environmental community so you can learn about their activities and strategies.

▌ Attend city council and planning board meetings.

▌ Listen to debates between members and the audience.

▌ Hear what people say and watch how the politicians vote.

▌ Observe how developers are treated by the decision-makers.

Get to know your local city council or county board members, the mayor or executive, and other local leaders. Call them to set up a meeting. Be insistent if they seem inaccessible. You have every right to lobby for your project and to meet directly with people to try to get them on your side. When you meet with each of your community's leaders, let them know about your proposed plans, and see what kind of response you get.

Even though you're not yet ready to apply for a zoning change or permits, it's still important to meet your local officials. Get to know them on a first-name basis. You'll have a lot more clout later on, when it counts.

Meet the decision-makers to learn about their "vision" of where the community is going. If they see development as a spur to more jobs, higher incomes, and overall economic growth, then let them know about *your* vision and how your project will contribute to the big picture.

It's also valuable to know up front which officials are firmly against growth and development. You can literally count votes against your project ahead of time by spending some time talking to those folks. And you can judge the overall political mood by looking at the support those people get at election time. This kind of information tells you whether or not your development idea makes *political* sense. If it doesn't, you're probably just wasting your time.

Your Side of the Story ...	The Argument Against ...
This project will improve the local economy by bringing in family-wage jobs.	This project is a threat to our way of life and to the character of our community.
You have performed exhaustive environmental reviews and studies in order to satisfy current legal requirements.	The developer has hired many experts, but all the studies in the world don't change the truth (as we see it).
The increased tax base will help improve the quality of local schools.	Increased traffic will endanger the lives of our children.

Figure 2-1 Both sides of the story

Who Calls the Shots?

You can easily identify your elected or appointed community leaders, but that might not be enough. In some communities the *real* leaders aren't necessarily the ones with the titles. You need to find out who *really* runs things. The best source for this information is from other builders — even your competitors.

Go to building association meetings, Chamber of Commerce meetings and social gatherings, and charity events that other developers may attend. Talk to them and get their opinions about who controls local decisions on growth and land use issues.

Develop a Political Strategy

You might not want to deal in politics, but sometimes you'll have to "play the game" with the local NIMBY group and their supporters. To do that, you'll have to meet those people in their own arena, which unfortunately is political.

Figure 2-1 is a table that demonstrates what you might encounter. On the left is evidence in favor of your project. On the right are the arguments you'll hear from the opposition.

Your side of the story is based on logical arguments. Attractive jobs, responsible environmental compliance, and increased future tax base are facts that you can prove. However, these arguments don't have the emotional power of the responses. Those arguments carry weight because they arouse sympathy and are easy to sell politically.

Emotional Arguments vs. Supply and Demand

Political arguments can affect the supply and demand cycle. The cycle is a real economic condition, and you have to know what phase it's in when you time critical business decisions. In the long run, nothing stops the cycle of supply and demand. But political strife over growth can skew the timing and make your job harder.

The reality of the supply and demand cycle can be overshadowed by strong opinions on either side of the growth issue.

In a perfect world, everyone, including local decision-makers, would be aware of the realities of the cycle. Planners would anticipate growth and then encourage development and entice employers to the area to accommodate that growth. But the reality of the supply and demand cycle can be overshadowed by strong opinions on either side of the growth issue.

If you try to take advantage of high-demand conditions when growth opponents are in the driver's seat, your efforts might work against you. Even when there's a hungry market for development, anti-growth political leaders won't respond positively to your evidence of high demand. They consider high demand a problem. You'll receive a very cool reception at the planning department. After all, you're one of those evil developers who caused that problem in the first place.

However, any politician in office who's gone through a budget cycle knows it's essential to improve tax revenues. Although they may be on the side of no-growth, politicians have to be realistic and look at the needs of the entire community. They know that opposing growth means revenues stagnate and public services decline. They can't take that stand forever and stay in office. Eventually they have to allow growth in order to promote a healthy economic environment.

Resist the Political Waves

How can you best approach political resistance? When politicians on either side of the growth issue are likely to ignore supply and demand realities, what information will help you get your project approved if you need a variance, rezone, conditional use permit, or some other change in zoning or land use?

Dedicate land for public use.
Solicit favorable publicity.
Demonstrate that you're sensitive to the environment.
Sell your case to no-growth advocates.

The answer is to find ways to get politicians to back your project. For example, you need to convince the anti-growth council member or planning commissioner that by voting for your plan, he or she remains faithful to that agenda. Let the elected official share the credit for your ideas. You'll get a lot of mileage out of letting the official get political points. That helps you because the formerly-hostile officials may now support — and want their names identified with — your plan.

Accentuate the positive. Include and emphasize parts of your plan that the slow-growth supporters like.

▌ Dedicate part of your land for public use, perhaps by adding a park or bicycle trail.

▌ Share your ideas with a sympathetic elected official and come up with ways to get some positive publicity. Try to get the local newspaper to run a human interest story about you — the developer who's voluntarily building a new park for the neighborhood kids.

▌ Many jurisdictions require setbacks and reserves for wetlands. Be generous. Provide more open space than you have to. Then be sure your local newspaper and planning department know what you're doing. This will be valuable ammunition later, if any anti-growth groups try to sabotage your development. You can assume the noble position of the good citizen who does more than the law requires, and that defeats the environmentalist's arguments.

▌ Invest in the community in a real way. Clean up and restore a creek, protect a wetland or habitat, and go beyond environmental requirements. Pay for an Environmental Impact Statement (EIS) without being forced to do so if you expect a lot of opposition to your plan. Many anti-growth groups go to court appealing approved development ideas with environmental arguments. Doing the EIS ahead of time defuses that bomb and puts you in the position of "good guy."

▌ Meet with the leaders of known anti-growth groups. Demonstrate how your project will enhance the area, upgrade the quality of life, and improve existing conditions. Ask to be allowed to speak at their next public meeting. Again, don't forget to alert a reporter from the local paper. When you present your case to anti-growth groups, publicity invariably works *for* you, even if they give you a hard time.

When the Sea Is Too Stormy

If the local leaders simply won't budge, you may have to reconsider before you proceed further. There's no sense in taking on a fight you can't afford, so you're wise to assess the battleground before you march onto it. If you face a truly hostile local government, here are some options:

1. Attempt to negotiate an acceptable compromise with your opponents. Be cautious, however. Don't make any promises you don't fully intend to keep. And get any concessions from *them* in writing. Growth opponents may seem agreeable in an effort to placate you, but then "forget" their implied support when it comes time to approve a rezone or issue permits.

2. Change your plan to a different one that fits with acceptable local themes.

Dave considers the possibility that he may have underestimated the
resources of the local no-growth group.

3. Delay your plan until the next election and work hard to help pro-growth candidates get elected.

4. Consider a different community. Sometimes a neighboring city will be eager to have you work with them to improve *their* economy.

This is not to say that you should always yield to a well-organized opposition group. On the contrary, be willing to fight to maintain your business and to exercise your rights. But before you spend money to buy land and create a development plan, be sure you know what lies ahead.

The Land Market

Before you start drawing plans for your new development, it's wise to make sure you haven't overlooked any options that might work even better for you. Begin by checking out the inventory of available land in your area, and see where the best buys are.

Perhaps the most expensive way to get land is to buy the cheapest acreage possible.

It isn't enough to know that there's land *available* for sale. You need to know how much and what kind it is, where it is, and whether it's appropriate for the use you have in mind. And most important: Can you buy it at a price that will let you make money on your project?

Your first step is to identify the available land. You probably won't find much if you're looking in midtown Manhattan. But there's a lot of raw land in West Texas. So if you live in New York City, should you saddle up and head west? Probably not. A big factor that determines the cost of raw land is the availability (or lack) of services.

Perhaps the most expensive way to get land is to buy the cheapest acreage possible. Why? Because you'll probably pay an arm and a leg to run basic services to it. The land is cheap because services aren't there yet, and in fact may be some distance away. As utilities, roads, and other services move closer to raw land, its value goes up.

Land with services in place or nearby will surely be more expensive than a similar parcel 20 miles out of town. But it might be a lot cheaper in the long run. You have to carefully consider whether it's cheaper to buy property with services already in place, or provide them yourself.

If you're looking at land that has no services installed, get estimates up front from your utility district, telephone, cable, electric and gas companies, and public works department. When you add it up, you could find that running services to supply the parcel you're considering works out to thousands of dollars per foot of frontage.

Utilities are usually installed in the access next to properties. So if the county has to run a five-mile sewer line, and your property fronts on a quarter mile of that route, you'll pay 1/20th of the total cost.

The trick to acquiring raw land is to identify the precise moment of opportunity. That's when basic services are available nearby, but the value of the land hasn't yet gone up as a result.

Remember that picking the right land market isn't the same as picking the right land.

As you begin your inventory of available land, look for parcels in the path of progress — in an area toward which current development is moving. But be aware that the path of progress doesn't always follow a constant course. It might change direction, or even stop cold (at least temporarily) just as it approaches the area you're considering. Even so, you can find real bargains in raw land if you recognize that path before anyone else is even aware of the changes that represent progress. So with this in mind, you need to study conditions and trends in the land market.

Remember that picking the right land *market* isn't the same as picking the right *land*. (We'll cover that in Chapter 4.) Just like any commodity, land varies in its attractiveness to investors, and that changes over time.

When you invest in the stock market, the price of a particular stock usually rises or falls within a limited range every day. When more people want the stock, it goes up. And when there are more sellers than buyers, the price goes down again.

This simplified description applies to all markets, including the market for land. But the stock market is a public auction marketplace that's active and easy to observe. While the same principles apply to the land market, the effects aren't as visible, the market isn't as flexible, and changes aren't as quick.

There are some popular myths about the land market. But there's no historical information to support them. Let's examine the following:

Myth: Land values always rise.

Fact: Land values do *not* always rise. They're just like stocks. If you invest in land that nobody else wants, and you can't improve it in some way to make it more attractive to buyers, you'll "lose your shirt" as the saying goes.

Myth: Changes in the land market are a direct reflection of developer activity.

Fact: Developers don't create land markets, they take advantage of them. Successful developers recognize emerging trends and take calculated risks to profit from those trends. You need to analyze growth patterns objectively and capitalize on potential by grabbing well-priced land before your competition notices its inherent value.

Myth: Land speculators significantly distort land values.

Fact: Speculation doesn't cause changes in land value. Instead, speculation is a direct result of changes in the land market. Don't fall for the myth that speculation is the cause. That's like Roger Blough's 1967 observation about inflation in Forbes magazine: "Steel prices cause inflation like wet sidewalks cause rain." If speculators could make land values rise, every landowner would hire a speculator!

Supply and Demand

The land market works like any other market. Its supply and demand cycle repeats in a predictable way (although not always on a predictable schedule).

Land prices don't rise and fall like the stock market, but rather reach price plateaus from which they rise again at the next turn of the cycle. This happens in direct response to the balance between the number of people who want to sell and those who want to buy.

Here are the phases of the supply and demand cycle for land:

1. **Demand is low**. Few buyers are in the market. Land available for sale just sits there.

2. **Demand increases**. Developers begin to compete for land in response to trends in population growth and commercial and industrial expansion. They gobble up every plot, lot and parcel.

3. **Supply increases**. More land becomes available as owners and speculators release it into the market.

4. **Demand begins to fall**. The market becomes saturated as available parcels exceed the number of potential buyers.

5. **Supply slows in response**. Properties don't sell as quickly as before. Some plots are withdrawn and new properties are slower to appear on the market.

Studying real estate cycles is somewhat like watching a horse race.

Of course, the stock market adage — buy low and sell high — applies here, too. The trick is to get into the land market at the *best* time for your project. But when is that?

It's easier to observe past real estate cycles than to recognize the exact phase of one when you're in the middle of it. As small indicators change, you can't be sure whether they signal a cycle change, or just a blip on the screen. Cycle timing is always different. A particular cycle can last a few months — or stretch out over a decade or more.

Economic conditions in *your* area will always dictate your financial success in buying and developing land. Those conditions also control the *speed* of the land market cycle.

Studying real estate cycles is somewhat like watching a horse race. A lot of unknown influences can change the outcome, making it impossible to predict with absolute accuracy. Cycles within a particular region have a rhythm of their own. Some revolve quickly, others more slowly. Cycle timing also changes with major population changes. Still, your best forecast will be based on a study of past cycles, tempered by knowledge of evolving economic and population trends.

Sometimes developers have a blind spot at the peak of the cycle. They often fail to recognize the gradual change in supply and demand as it occurs, because their emphasis is on developing and marketing more units. They're more likely to see potential for business on the up side of the cycle, and less likely to see the slowdown and pending change on the down side.

It's probably fair to say that if you buy land in an economically-expanding region, you'll eventually make money — if you're willing to wait long enough. But most of us need to turn over our investment capital, sell our project, and pay off the financing within a limited time. We don't have the capital to wait out what could be a very long cycle. So you need to look for important clues about where the cycle sits right now. These include:

▌ **The current housing inventory**. If your community has more than a year's supply of housing available, the market is extremely soft. If it's less than three months' supply, the market is hot. But don't look at today's number alone. Study trends over the past two or three years.

▌ **An analysis of other construction.** Housing is a good indicator regardless of the project you have in mind. If you want to develop land for industrial or commercial use, you need a growing population to supply employees and customers. So if housing sales are slow or heading downward, that's negative. If contractors can't build houses quickly enough for the demand, then you have a positive indicator.

▌ **What your competitors are doing.** Are other contractors and developers busily pursuing big plans? Or are they idle? They're looking at the same evidence you are, so their activities reflect their "take" on the supply and demand cycle.

One word [...] where you get opinions about local conditions: Real [...] toriously optimistic. They make a living from [...] ke to predict that the next big boom is just ab[...]

Land

Fe[...] also affect supply and demand. Not only that, [...] ath of future development.

[...] be developed only so far. Once land on the [...] values go up. By comparison, an area with [...] ons with ample water supply and a slow-to-[...] ts no compelling and immediate reason for [...] land inventory and growth potential are virtu-

[...] ly mean that buying up a couple hundred acres for [...] ove. It's true that when there's a lot of cheap land availab[...] ter flexibility and choice. But be sure the availability of land is [...] d by the availability of buyers for what you want to develop. We'll discuss that in more detail later in this chapter.

Remember that some part of almost any parcel will be required for environmental mitigation in virtually any kind of project. Be sure you know the setback rules in your area, and don't assume they're the same for every kind of development. If you've always done residential building, you need to

---

It's entirely possible that one-third or more of the total land area won't be available for your project.

find out how the rules differ for industrial or commercial projects. Everything could be different.

Wetland regulations vary, depending on the type of land, the type of project, and the lay of the land and habitat. You'll need to hire an environmental specialist to help you prepare an Environmental Impact Statement and determine requirements for wetland and habitat reserves. If creeks or rivers run through the property, you'll probably have to allow setbacks on both shores all the way through. It's entirely possible that one-third or more of the total land area won't be available for your project. Be sure to consider all this when you study the land inventory. And don't forget to take these things into account when you compare raw land costs.

Where to Find Information

Even in your own area, what's going on in the land market now and what will probably occur in the near future aren't always obvious. You need to search a bit to identify the current status of the market for available land.

Track the *spread* between listed prices and actual selling prices by quarter over the past two years. The spread is a percentage you can calculate by subtracting the sales price from the asked price, then dividing the result by the asked price. For example:

Asking price	$100,000
Selling price	$90,000
Difference	$10,000
Spread	10,000 divided by 100,000 equals **0.10** percent

The greater the spread, the softer the market.

Also find out how long properties remain on the market in the zoning class you're considering.

These tests will give you a fairly reliable indication of the strength or weakness of the land market. If the spread between listed and selling prices is small (5 percent or less), that means that demand is sharp for those types of properties. Buyers are willing to offer at or near asked prices, and chances are that a lot of buyers are shopping right now. But it's a sign of weakness if the spread is over 10 percent or so. Demand is low and sellers are forced to accept deeply discounted offers in order to sell.

These signs are fairly reliable for residential properties, but less certain for commercial and industrial development sites. In those situations, you need to study the current lands inventory which lists details (acreage, location, zoning and included services) about available properties. Many counties and cities develop these inventories.

Study industrial and commercial lands using the following tests in addition to the spread between asked and selling price:

▌ How many of the lands identified on the inventory are relatively small (plots of one acre or less)? These are probably not good development candidates and should be taken off your list of "available" lands even if they could be combined to make a parcel big enough for your use. Adjoining small plots present special problems of their own. Each separate owner may have very different plans for their properties, so acquiring them might be difficult. Just because similarly-zoned properties lie adjacent to one other doesn't make them "available." Planners may not see it that way, but that's the reality for developers.

▌ How many of the lands identified are pocket-zoned, meaning that nonconforming zoning is grandfathered in but surrounded by properties with a different zoning class? Chances are high that undeveloped nonconforming lands *aren't* practical in terms of development potential. The only exception would be if your area is one in which grandfather clauses protecting nonconforming land use expire upon sale of the property, so the parcel automatically assumes the zoning defined by the surrounding property when it's sold.

▌ How many acres in the inventory are already developed? Sometimes these appear in the lands inventory by mistake.

▌ How many acres *aren't* for sale? Remember that just because land has a particular zoning class doesn't mean that's the way the owner wants to use it, or that they're interested in selling.

▌ Ask your county officials what they consider to be the number of years' supply represented by current inventory. Your own analysis, with the points above in mind, might reveal that a county's expectations are unrealistic. You might conclude that what is described as a "50-year supply" actually will be used up in five to 10 years — not an uncommon situation at all.

▌ Finally, see if there's a steady relationship (within a particular zoning class) between the number of acres that come up for sale each year and the *total* acreage covered in the lands inventory. If that ratio remains fairly steady (the inventory keeps growing), chances are good that the land for sale each year is a dependable indicator of future supply.

Check the sources listed below for more current and detailed information for all types of land. Remember, finding information for residential land is fairly easy. Banks, real estate agents, and lenders usually know that market well. But you may need to study zoning maps, neighborhood plans, countywide plans, and other documents to dig out the real nitty-gritty on nonresidential property. Here's a list to get you started:

▌ The Multiple Listing Service office or any real estate firm belonging to the MLS is a good source for statistical information about sales trends and available properties.

▌ Business and economics departments at local universities and colleges publish studies of land use trends and other economic statistics that go back over many years.

▌ Planning agencies, local, regional and state, will provide details and clarification of zoning issues.

▌ Check with the State Environmental Protection Agency. Introduce yourself at the local office. You'll be dealing with those officials when your project comes up for environmental review. It doesn't hurt to get information at the beginning about what might be expected of you.

▌ Land rights groups might be aware of local legal battles that could affect the local market.

▌ Building industry associations are excellent networking sources for meeting other developers and contractors whose knowledge and experience can help you. If you don't already belong, join one.

▌ Try the Internet. Ask around and check the phone book and newspaper ads for Web site addresses for the groups and agencies above. Start with your planning department, economic development agency and Chamber of Commerce. Their Web sites often have links to other local agencies and groups and can save you a lot of research time.

Other sources of information include union offices, building exchange offices, and the local private classified phone directories, which may have bigger and more informative ads than the telephone company's edition.

Introduce your project.

Figure 2-2 is a sample introductory letter you can send to various organizations to "grease the skids" before you contact them in person.

When you call for the appointment, be specific about the kind of information you're looking for. The individual or agency may already have printed materials that cover exactly what you want. Ask if they have handouts or brochures that describe their services or resources. Some organizations may offer materials for sale. Ask about that when you call, so the person you're meeting can have those materials ready for you when you arrive.

[Date]

[Title, First Name, Last Name]

[Company or organization]

[Street]

[City, State, Zip]

Dear [Title] [Last Name]:

I'm surveying the land market in [city and county] with the intent to find property to develop into [briefly describe your project]. My research indicates that there's a good market for this project idea right now.

As a first step, I want to gauge the availability of land in this area for my purpose, and I'd like to ask you to help me by suggesting areas you believe are best suited for this project, and perhaps referring me to resources for information I'll need before I proceed.

I want to be especially sensitive to local concerns about environmental and quality-of-life questions. For that reason, I'm starting out by contacting knowledgeable leaders like yourself for input and reactions to my plan.

I'll call within the next few days to ask for an appointment so we can meet briefly to discuss my project. I believe my plans will add vitality and economic benefit to the community, and I hope you'll agree. I look forward to meeting you.

Sincerely,

[Your name and signature]

Figure 2-2 Sample introductory letter

The General Plan

The general plan is a blueprint for a community's future growth.

Get a copy of the general plan for your area. This may be called a neighborhood plan, comprehensive plan, sub-area plan, land-use plan or some other name. It defines the guidelines for development and growth.

The plan varies by community. General plans are developed with considerable public input (if the public is interested) or in a complete vacuum (if the public simply doesn't think it affects them).

Either way, it's usually a highly-detailed description of planning goals and policies, organized by neighborhoods and areas. It's a blueprint for the entire community and reflects the official vision for the future growth of

Dave was surprised at the resistance he met when he applied for a zoning variance for the wrecking yard he had planned.

the community. It will include extensive descriptions of required zoning and development limitations, and detailed zoning maps.

You can get a complete copy of your local plan, usually for photocopying costs. A diskette may be available for $10 to $20, which is easier to handle and to read than a pile of paper.

The plan shows where each type of growth will be allowed, often by mapped-out "urban growth boundaries" according to estimated needs over the next 10 to 20 years. If the plan was done properly, it will also show where nonresidential growth will be allowed and will tie in with a lands inventory. (If it *wasn't* done properly, this could be a perfect opportunity for you to take the lead in influencing the direction for your community's growth by initiating improvements to the general plan. We'll discuss that further in the next chapter.)

The general plan will be valuable tool to help you focus on the best areas for your development type when you begin to look for available land.

Zoning Laws

Visit your planning department and become familiar with your local zoning ordinances. The zoning laws affect everything you plan to do. Before you buy land, you need to know what the rules are going to be. You can get copies of these ordinances, usually for the cost of duplication, either on paper or computer disk.

Find out how available property is zoned by referring to your general plan documents or checking with your planning department. You also need to know which properties are currently eligible for rezoning, and if so, to what degree.

All these steps will help you confirm that your development idea is feasible, and that suitable land is available.

How to Report Land Values and Trends

When you go to the bank for a loan, be prepared to educate and inform. Never assume that a banker knows everything about the local land market. It's your job to give them that information.

Remember that bankers are experts on money, not development. They're fairly comfortable with the residential market because they deal largely with mortgage loans. But don't assume they know about development — particularly commercial or industrial. You may have to educate them about local land economics and characteristics that you've encountered in your search for your project site. That's where your land market report comes in, no matter what kind of development project you undertake.

Here are the questions you'll need to answer before you prepare the land market study you'll include in your business plan:

- How much land is available for your type of project? (Total acreage, number of plots.)
- Where is each parcel? (Key each property to a map.)
- How big is it?
- How is it currently zoned?
- How is it being used now?
- What requirements exist for buffers, open space, habitats, etc.?
- Prospects for rezoning if necessary?
- Who owns it?
- What is the owner's intention for the land?
- How much does it cost?
- Who owns parcels that aren't on the market, but might be suitable for your development plans?

The answer to this last question might not prove very useful. But you can always approach owners directly and make an offer on land that isn't for sale. They could be receptive if your timing (and the price) is right. If the property is owned by a local or state government, you'll have to face the bureaucratic maze, starting with the local land trust office or agency that has title to the land. This can be tough. Governments often acquire land, but rarely like to give it up again.

You'll probably find several possible sites for your project. Figure 2-3 is a two-page format you can use to gather and organize information about the land inventory. Use the first page for analysis of the available sites, and the second to expand your information about restrictions to development, and services and amenities available at the property.

A thorough analysis of the land market in your area will tell you if your community is the best place to buy raw land for your development. If not, you'd be better off taking your project elsewhere.

Once you've found a "friendly" land market, then record your findings in detail. You and your lender both want to know how you determined that you've picked the best location for your plan.

Your Market

Let's assume that you've found that your project won't draw unreasonable political resistance and there's affordable land available. Your next step is to prepare a detailed argument that proves there will be buyers for your development when it's finished.

Nothing gives a potential lender more confidence than being approached by a business owner who knows who his buyers are, and how to sell them what they want. In the rest of this chapter you'll see how to gather the information that will convince a lender that you are the expert on your market.

Bankers know about money. But they may not be experts on the land market, or on the buyer's market for your proposed development. You need to convince your loan officer of the merits of your project by presenting numbers and facts that prove your idea is a *profitable* one. You do that by proving that demand for your finished product is strong and likely to continue growing.

Remember that money — like all commodities — is limited, and lenders have to make choices about the best way to invest it. That's where you have an edge. Your market study, attached to your business plan, will help convince your lender to choose *you* and your project as a desirable investment.

Why do you need both a business plan and a market study? Because they serve different purposes. The business plan focuses on your business — financial statements, forecasts, budgets and the all-important *pro forma* estimate which predicts how the project will affect your bottom line. The market study is a compilation of statistics that deal with your competition, the demand factors that bring in buyers for your project and ensure your profit, political influences on real estate development, and the economic and demographic conditions and trends in your area.

Available Land Analysis

Total suitable available acres: _____   Number of plots: _____

Site location	Size (acres)	Zoning	Current use	Owner	Cost per acre

Figure 2-3 Available land analysis

Available Land Analysis

Site	1	2	3	4	5	6	7	8	9	10
Location										
Exempt										
Building acres										
Services present										
Water										
Gas										
Electricity										
Telephone										
Cable										
Amenities available										
School										
Hospital										
Fire										
Police										
Trash handling										
Street maintenance										
Public area maintenance										

Figure 2-3 Available land analysis (continued)

Here's how the process *should* go:

▮ You want to develop a small tract of homes or an industrial complex.

▮ You begin with an idea and start looking into the possibilities.

▮ You check out land prices and discover that demand is on the way up, but that raw land prices are still relatively low.

▮ The political climate is positive, little competition exists for the development you have in mind, and there are buyers eager for such properties.

▮ Finally, lenders are ready to finance land and development projects.

If all this is true, then you should proceed at once.

But in real life we often find that not all these encouraging circumstances are in place at the same time. You need to assess the risks involved with your plans, then alter your project if necessary to accommodate a less-than-ideal market. You stand a much better chance of succeeding when you've studied the market at the beginning of the process. That way you know up front what your obstacles may be.

Preliminary Suggestions

Become a market expert.
Write the market
study yourself.
Describe the risks as well
as potential profits.
Base the entire plan
on facts.
Use graphics.

If you want your market study to shine, simply pack it with up-to-date, accurate, relevant information, explain that information clearly, and lead the reader through the report so that the connection between the information and your project is obvious.

If referenced materials are too bulky, don't attach them, just refer to them and cite them properly. Make them available on request.

Don't depend too much on national statistics. Those may be quite outdated for your purpose and could have little to do with local conditions.

Write the market study yourself. To prepare a market study, you need to know all the facts and risks that contribute to the big picture. If you hire someone else to do this for you, you won't have the direct knowledge and insight you need to make you the real expert, which is what you should be.

An objective market study frankly explores not only the potential for success, but also the risk of failure. You may think you should paint as optimistic a picture as possible and avoid any mention of potential risks. A banker knows there's no such thing as a perfect, risk-free project, and if you pretend yours is, he may think you're letting your enthusiasm for your idea cloud your judgment. A complete discussion of risk should be a prominent part of your market study. Admit that "Here are ways my plan could fail," but follow through with, "Here's how I plan to manage these risks."

Dave wonders if hiring his wife's brother to do the market research for
potential development sites was such a good idea.

Project your ideas and hopes with solid, appropriate, and timely information. Get your facts from objective sources:

❚ Local or regional polling data and demographic studies. Make sure statistics you quote are current. You need to know what's happened in the past year in order to forecast the future. If the latest population or employment numbers are three years old, they tell you nothing about the next year or two.

❚ Your state employment or human resources development office is a good source for current employment information. Their numbers are usually updated quarterly.

❚ Your local public library. The reference librarian can often give you access to a volume which lists every company in your area by classification, including their address, telephone number, number of years in business, and the names of owners or officers. They also have similar listings for public agencies and organizations.

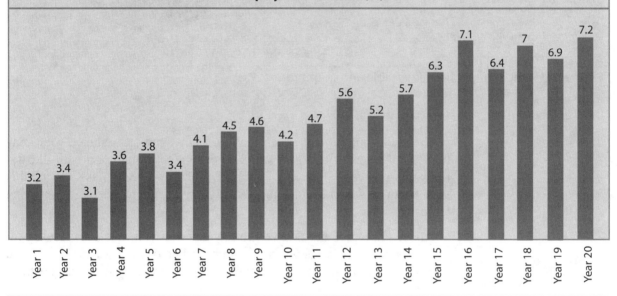

Narrative description

Our community is growing. Housing construction has enjoyed a healthy climate for the past 20 years, with relatively steady demand throughout that period. Slow-downs have occurred in conjunction with the cycle of job market demand. However, employment has risen each year over the past twenty years, with no less than a 3 percent increase every year and some years showing as much as 7 percent growth.

Graphic description

The following graph shows the percentage by which employment has increased over the last 20 years, leading to a steady demand for housing construction.

Employment Increase (%)

Figure 2-4 Bar graph illustration

▌ Local political offices, including those of the mayor, city, county and state legislators. Besides helping you to understand and respond to local anti-growth issues, these offices are good sources for economic and marketing statistics.

Be careful when you make assumptions based on historical analysis. You need to show a strong correlation between historical events and present conditions. Look for trends and not just statistics of the moment.

Use illustrations. When you present statistics and trends, put these on a graph or chart instead of burying them in narrative. Figure 2-4 shows a sample page from a market study that includes both text and a bar graph to furnish data.

Rows and columns of numbers don't make very interesting reading, either. Figure 2-5 shows a table that shows employment statistics about a community, and a graph that shows the same thing.

Occupation	Number	Percent of Total
Executive	59,032	13.36
Professional	66,412	15.03
Technical/Clerical	91,204	20.64
Sales	55,709	12.61
Services	57,078	12.92
Production	46,962	10.63
Other	65,388	14.80
Total	441,785	100.00

Figure 2-5 Employment figures in table and graph formats

Graphics simplify your presentation. They show at a glance what may take many pages of text to relate. Hire someone to help you with illustrations if you have to. But your computer probably already has software that will let you make some amazing-looking graphs and tables by just entering the data.

Above all, remember that you're the expert in your business. Trust your own judgment. You've done the research, and no one knows better than you what will work, whether it will make money, and that you're qualified to do it.

The Format of the Study

Work from summary to detail.

Make your reader's job easy.

Reference your resources.

Choose an order that makes sense.

Stick to the subject.

Make it brief.

Begin by organizing the information you've collected into logical sections. You can be pretty informal at this point. But when you prepare the final copy to attach to your business plan, make it easy for the lender or investor to read and understand. Just like with a building, start with the foundation, frame it in, and then top it off.

Here are my recommendations:

1. Start with a one-page summary, where you condense each section of your study into a sentence or two. You want your reader to absorb the essential conclusions of your report on page 1 — and in 30 seconds or less. Include page numbers in the summary or include a table of contents. Readers can turn to the detail section if they want more detail.

2. Make the report simple and easy to read. Leave lots of white space. Make it as short as you can. Include distinct headings so main topics are easy to find and review.

3. Attach captions to charts and graphs, and show where you got the information. It's better to include references in the text of the report than to put them in footnotes or in a list at the end of the report, where the reader would have to search for them. For captions, references or footnotes (if you *must* use them), show the author's name, title of the report or article, publication date and page number. Indicate which source materials are attached to the study, and have the other sources organized and readily available if the reader requests them.

4. Consider arranging your report according to the "hot buttons" you want to emphasize — with the hottest ones first. For example, if it's likely land prices are about to surge, start with that. If a major employer has just announced they're moving to your area, start with employment opportunities and demographics. Otherwise, follow my recommendations below.

5. The report should address only market conditions. The lender's interest in the report grows from this all-important question: "Are there buyers for this project who can pay what it takes for the developer to make money?"

The elegance of a clearly-stated point is always more powerful than an unnecessarily lengthy discussion. If you have a report that shows employment is rising in your community, summarize it in a single paragraph or chart as evidence of a healthy market for housing, jobs, or commercial or industrial development. Reference the source, then move on.

What to Include in the Study

Figure 2-6 is a checklist to help you prepare your market study. These are the things you'll have to learn about before you become the expert your lender expects you to be.

The market study has to include at least the following information:

Your competition.
Trends for your development class.
Local demographics and economy.
Politics and your market.
Risk management.
The timing.

Your Competition

Competition defines a healthy market. A market doesn't exist without competition. If only one company offers a particular product or service, they can charge anything they want. The buyer has no other options.

On the other hand, excessive competition within a limited market spells trouble for all but the strongest competitors. If there are many companies in your area doing the kind of development you're considering, you need to demonstrate to your lender that your business will be among the successful ones.

Your competition
❏ Who are your competitors?
❏ Are they more or less experienced than you?
❏ Are your competitors better or worse off financially than you?
❏ What is their annual sales volume?
❏ How many people do they employ?
❏ What are their specialties?

Trends for your development class
❏ How many homes like yours are already for sale?
❏ How long do they stay on the market?
❏ Who's buying them?
❏ How much are buyers paying for them?
❏ Are buyers paying close to the asking price?
❏ Which age segment of the population are you targeting?
❏ How many of those people are there?

Local demographics and economy
❏ Are population centers shifting in your area?
❏ How many people are moving to or away from your community?
❏ What's the breakdown of income levels among local residents?
❏ How many and what kinds of jobs are available?
❏ How does the population break down by age?
❏ Which age brackets are significantly growing or decreasing?
❏ How do assessed values for land and improvements compare to those nearby?
❏ Analyze crime rates by location.
❏ What's the current status of industrial and commercial development?

Politics and your market
❏ Will environmentalists resist your plan?
❏ What's the ratio between pro-growth and no-growth backers in city/county government?
❏ Are planners cooperative with developers?
❏ Is there an active movement to attract new business to the area?

Risk management
❏ Are there enough potential buyers earning enough to buy your houses?
❏ Are interest rates rising, dropping, or remaining stable?
❏ Are there signs pointing to an upcoming economic decline?

Figure 2-6 Market study checklist

It's easier than you might think to get information about your competitors. Contractors tend to be open about their gross receipts, even when their net income isn't all that impressive.

You can easily find out the amounts of winning bids (and the names of the successful contractors). Local newspapers or business journals publish this information to let all bidders know where they stood in the rankings. These listings at least tell you the gross on major jobs. Your local builder's exchange may provide summaries of both private and publicly-bid projects for their members.

If your competitors are incorporated, you can get their annual reports either directly or from a stock exchange broker. You can also find them on the Internet by searching for "annual report." If you have a company's trading symbol, you can get their annual report at no charge from Barron's by calling 800-965-2929, or by fax to 800-747-9384.

You can also tell a lot by comparative employment studies. If one contractor hires more people than all the rest put together, it's safe to gauge competitive standing on the basis of the numbers of people each company employs. You can get employment figures from your library's industrial source directory, from Chambers of Commerce, economic development agencies, state employment offices, and the companies themselves.

Trends for Your Development Class

A study of recent market trends may reveal some risks you haven't considered.

Example: Your plan is to develop 50 new homes in the price range between $150,000 and $200,000. But in that range many homes have been on the market for a long time. On average, they end up selling for $30,000 below the asking price. Families are buying homes in a range $50,000 lower than your target, and supply is much greater than demand with no change in sight.

With evidence of such trends in hand, a lender would be justified in discouraging you from continuing with your plans. The timing is simply not right for what you have in mind. The smart move is to wait until market conditions favor your plan. Or find a more vigorous market and change your plan to fit that market.

But if trends show that there will be buyers clamoring for your development, lenders will be much more at ease about your potential for financial success. Make sure your study shows indications of a strong market now and in the near future.

Local Demographics and Economy

Some of the same resources you used for the land market study can help you here. Check with real estate offices, moving companies, the police department, school board, city hall, the Chamber of Commerce, planning department, treasurer, assessor, and tax collector. These agencies can provide you with the facts and figures you need to show local demographic and economic trends.

Your challenge is to summarize all this information into a clear, concise and easy-to-understand report that supports your claim that buyers are present and ready for your project.

Politics and Your Market

> *The reality of the supply and demand cycle can be overshadowed by strong opinions on either side of the growth issue.*

Briefly describe the local political climate and how it affects your market. Do community leaders invite new employers to the area and encourage development, housing and amenities to support their employees? Or is there a no-growth sentiment that may hamper your efforts to get zoning changes and permits? Show recent city council and planning commission voting records on issues concerning projects similar to yours. Is it apparent that the pendulum is about to swing from one side to the other, either way?

If the planners and politicians are becoming more sympathetic to developers, you're looking at a rosy future. But if there's a threat that no-growth activists are gaining influence, you can make a case for striking quickly while the iron's hot to forge your development plans. This part of the market study helps convince the lender of your project's timeliness.

Risk Management

There are always risks involved when you're trying to sell something. And your lender is made painfully aware of that when a borrower defaults on a loan. You have to prove that you've considered the marketing risks and taken steps to prevent them from sinking your project. Here are some things to discuss under risk management:

▌ Declining demand resulting in lower prices. If the spread between asking and selling prices is increasing, this tells you that demand is softening, and buyers are confident that they can negotiate prices downward.

▌ Undercutting by competitors.

▌ Decline in the local economy — layoffs and business failures.

▌ Higher interest rates (for you if yours is a variable rate loan, or for your buyers).

Summarize how your market plan shows evidence that these risks (and others you may encounter) are minor, or that the plan allows for a reasonable profit even if some of these risks become reality.

Is the Timing Right?

That the timing is right for your project should be the concluding summary of your market study. Here's where you interpret the information you've presented. For example, if the spread between asking prices and selling prices is declining, explain how this shows that demand is picking up. A steady trend implies a healthy balance between supply and demand.

When you describe the building cycle, the interest rate cycle, and the economic cycle, mention international and national trends for comparison only. Let your lender know that you realize your world extends beyond your city limits and that you're aware of the influence of events in other places.

But emphasize that while national and worldwide trends and economic changes may affect you, they're not nearly as important as what's going on right down the street. What you pay for lumber, wages you pay to get skilled workers, what you pay in interest rates at the local bank, are far more important than exchange rates, crises in Europe or Asia, and economic cycles that are different from the ones you experience yourself. (Even nationally-set mortgage rates are irrelevant to the degree that local supply and demand ultimately determines how much you'll pay in interest.)

Regional trends are the ones that matter.

If your loan officer believes that international trends direct the economy, you need to show him or her that it's regional trends that really matter. It makes no difference if the national construction market is slow. If business is booming in your area, that's all that really counts.

You can see by looking at conditions around the country that what's happening in Ohio doesn't directly affect the local economy in West Texas or Seattle. Different parts of the country react differently to economic news and trends, depending on such things as their population, job opportunities and housing costs.

During your research you'll gather far more information than you'll publish in the market report. That's the value you receive from the research. Remember, the purpose of the market study you present to a lender is to convince them that you've done your homework, and that your plans for your project are based on reality, not just dreams.

Your job — not your lender's — is to become the expert not only on construction and development, but also on the condition of the market. And remember that "the market" consists of many parts, all of them driven by supply and demand. The market for land development is influenced not only by potential buyers, but by politics, building costs, competition, and the availability of the land itself. All parts of that market grow, retreat and change direction over time. It's like trying to stay ahead of a teenager. You have to constantly check, verify and check again to keep pace with it as it changes — and change can happen all too quickly.

Chapter 3

Development Alternatives

So far you've decided it's time to expand your business. You've asked a lot of questions, inspected the available land, and studied the demand for various kinds of development. But the door is still open to make sure your original plan is the best possible one.

Maybe residential development is hot in your area right now. You see other companies buying tracts of land and building large numbers of houses, so you think you'll try the same thing. But this might not be the best direction for your efforts if you don't have the experience or working capital. Or maybe the best available sites are already taken and those remaining are too expensive.

Don't tie yourself to a plan just because someone else has been successful with it. Review your options once more, especially if your market studies revealed less-than-perfect opportunities for your original plan.

You can't open a general store and expect to compete with Sears or Wal-Mart. So don't attempt to compete on terms dictated by the big guys in development and construction, either. You're better off finding a specialized development niche where you can excel.

The interesting thing about development is that so many possibilities are available. Don't be surprised to find that you start out assuming you want to follow one course, only to end up going a different way. Some would-be developers become pure speculators; others get rich going into long-term property management.

Land Speculation

One of the services speculators provide is to consolidate land for large-tract development. Now this isn't the same as composing a master plan. That's where several different owners join in the planning process for their properties. (We discuss that later in the chapter.) Here we address buying up several parcels and joining them into a singly-owned tract for development.

This is where a speculator can solve the problem. By buying up different owners' lands, the speculator can approach local planners with a large piece of land appropriate for rezoning. He can argue that not only is the consolidated parcel appropriate for development, it's also large enough to accommodate setbacks and environmental mitigation, factors that prevent most owners of small lots from seriously considering a big zoning change request, let alone a development plan.

> **Example:** In one area there are many small, individually-owned tracts of land that are suitable for development. The lots are now zoned either rural, agricultural or residential in nearly equal numbers. The area might be appropriate for industrial use, but no single owner or group of owners is motivated or able to organize the lots in question.

"Donut Holes" and LIDs

Planners don't like "donut holes" — pockets of undeveloped land in the path of progress. That's why they plan for development by designing Local Improvement Districts to assess property owners for improvements or utilities within a defined area. These can present an opportunity or a nuisance for you as a speculator, depending on your timing.

If you're holding land you bought earlier to consolidate small parcels into a larger one, you may be included in an LID before you're ready. But you could also use an LID as leverage to convince owners to sell their properties to you. Those owners may not want to pay for services just because surrounding owners do, and would prefer to sell their land rather than pay for the improvements.

Participation in an LID may be determined by a simple majority or by a land majority. In a simple majority, the number of owners voting for or against the LID determines whether it goes into effect. In a land majority, each landowner has as many votes as they have acres of land. That way, if you already own 250 acres within a proposed 400-acre district, you already have a majority of the votes. You'll pay for a proportionate share of the LID costs if the LID is formed.

In either case, small owners who oppose the district usually end up as reluctant participants if it passes. Sometimes they're allowed to opt out, but will have to pay a latecomer's fee once they sell the property or decide to join the LID.

Property owners are usually allowed to pay for LID improvements over several years with low-interest loans, so the financial impact doesn't hit all at once.

Financing for Speculation

People who recognize opportunities before everyone else are the ones who make the most money from investments. Land speculators see where the path of progress is headed, then they buy land while it's cheap and sell it at a handsome profit later.

But you're not likely to find a lender willing to advance you money for speculation in anything — land included.

You'll need ready cash to take advantage of fleeting opportunities unless you can raise money quickly. One option is to have potential investment partners lined up to act as general partners in a limited partnership that can be formed on short notice.

Another option is to work from a line of credit with a lender. You'll probably pay interest significantly higher than current market rates, but that might be OK if you're confident that you can depend on a good short-term profit through a quick turnaround on your investment.

Speculation Targets

If your city has started to expand outward into multi-use communities, you can see the direction the path of progress is taking and make some assumptions about future land uses.

Edge City development

The appearance of the Edge City (as this outward development is called) is characterized by the loss of a central urban identity. New commercial areas, including retail shopping malls and office parks, spring up on the edges instead of being confined to the core of the city. Planners see this as the "perfect" community, so they plan for new development to conform. Residential areas surround the shopping hubs. Commercial and light industrial areas are located farther out, with heavy-impact industrial zones farthest of all.

Planners view the Edge City as having a certain elegance. But it also lacks the charm found in mixed-use communities. And it turns everyone into commuters. There are no corner stores or movie theaters, and distances are often greater from homes to parks, schools, churches, shopping centers and work places than in the traditional core city.

Because of these nontraditional development patterns, past trends may not be as helpful in predicting the future as they once were. To succeed as a land speculator, you should study trends in nearby newly-developed areas and look for signs of similar changes in your area.

Look for evidence that:

▌ There's no reason for the path of progress to slow or change direction.

▌ The current political mood will remain favorable to development.

▌ There's nothing on the horizon to indicate that these circumstances will change dramatically in coming months.

From these you can probably assume that land you buy on speculation along the path of progress will increase in value. But be cautious. Remember that when you take big chances in land speculation, there's always the risk that you've judged the situation incorrectly or that conditions will change suddenly and unexpectedly.

Maybe you can buy low-priced, well-situated land, get it rezoned (to improve its value) and then develop it yourself for even more profit. But that's risky because you might run into opposition which could delay or even prevent the rezone. But if it works, this certainly would be one cheap way to get land for your future development plans.

You might invest in land with the intent of holding it. You're gambling that its value will increase over time, even if you don't do anything with it. This doesn't always happen, but sometimes you can be lucky enough to have someone come along and offer to buy you out at a nice profit.

But are you a speculator, a long-term investor, or a developer? If you're a developer, you want to put the land to work for you right away, build your project, and then move on to the next one.

Increase the Land Supply Inventory

There are other ways to develop land besides building houses, factories or stores on it. One way is to make the land more attractive to buyers or other developers. That also makes the land more valuable to you. While closely related, this differs from pure speculation because in this case you add value to the land. Even if you only get the zoning changed, the property value increases.

Getting financing for this type of development is like the chicken-and-egg question: Which comes first? Will a lender finance your costs to install basic services or apply for a rezone before the planning agencies approve the zoning change? Unfortunately, no. You'll have to get a firm commitment — in writing — before you can get a loan. That contract must provide that you'll get zoning approval without fail if you fulfill the contract requirements. You may have to go through a public hearing to get an ordinance passed declaring the rezone before the banker will even talk to you. That ordinance will probably include provisions that utilities be installed and paid for by a certain deadline.

The lender will also want to know how the rezone or improvements to the land will affect its value. For example, if the land is currently zoned rural, and you're going for a rezone to residential, it's pretty certain the land's value will go up as a result. Land for residential use is usually the most expensive. But there may be exceptions to this. In areas where there's demand for heavy industrial development, but little land available, that land value could go sky high if you can get it rezoned to industrial.

You might buy land for rezone and development, and then realize that you'll make more money (and save yourself a lot of hassle) by just selling it again right away. That makes sense if short-term profit matters more to you than the potential for greater profits later. Another choice is to hold the land, develop it, then manage it yourself for several years.

The disadvantage here is that you'll have to deal with tenant issues and it may take some time before the cash flow stream begins. That can be a problem if you have to pay back a large short-term loan. If you don't want to be involved in land management, you should probably build your project, sell it, take your profit, and move on.

Become Active in Land Use Planning

In your land study, you learned how land currently on the market is zoned. In your market study, you made some predictions about the future demand for various development types. That means you have the information you need to become an active planner in your area. If you can prove that not all available land with a particular zoning can be developed for that use, and that there's a market for that use, you can make a strong case for a rezone of more land for that use.

> **Example**: A builder wanted to develop a self-storage and warehousing center. He knew that those facilities were in short supply. They're relatively cheap to build and there's little tenant turnover. He applied to the planning department to get light industrial zoning on some agricultural land he had an option to buy. He was turned down despite the fact that the plot was suitable for that use. The planners claimed there was already a 10-year inventory of land zoned light industrial, so no rezones were being issued for that class.

The land supply figures were based on a comparison between past population and land use, and an estimate of future growth. But the planning department's assumptions were wrong. They included all land currently zoned industrial, believing that it would all be developed in the future. This developer got his rezone because he was able to prove that many of those parcels were:

▌ Too small for development

▌ Located on wetlands

▌ Lots left over from tracts developed earlier

▌ Attached to existing projects as buffer zones and could never be developed

That example shows that with a little research, you can (and should) challenge the planning department, and win.

Residential Development

Housing development can range from single-family homes built one by one, to huge tracts of hundreds or thousands of units. It also includes income properties (apartments or condominiums) and "second homes" (resort or vacation homes).

The market for residential development has sub-markets, like any other. As the baby boomers in your area retire and sell their homes, they'll release those properties for sale to younger families. At the same time, they'll look for lower-maintenance, and often smaller, housing for themselves.

If you live where winters are harsh, retirees may move elsewhere. But if you're in the sunbelt, older people from snowbelt places like Maine or North Dakota may flock like migratory birds to your part of the country. Take these factors into account when you consider the many and varied residential development alternatives.

Building a single house on spec is the way many people get into the residential development market. For a small construction company, that's an excellent way to begin. Some builders move into a spec house while they put on the finishing touches, then sell the property and use the profit to buy another lot and start all over again. Others have several houses in various stages of completion.

At this level, you're not as dependent on the market as you would be if you tried to sell dozens or hundreds of homes at once. It's fairly easy to sell a single custom home, even in the worst market. But if you're building several hundred homes while the market is slowing down, it could spell disaster for you, your project, and the lender. It makes sense to start out slowly because it makes financing easier — there's less risk for the lender.

Expect to put up 30 percent of the cost to develop residential property yourself.

Lenders are usually more comfortable with housing than with nonresidential development. Supply and demand cycles for commercial or industrial properties may be more of a mystery to them.

Most lenders understand the housing market, at least from the point of view of mortgage banking. They know that the way to lend money is to be sure the borrower has some stake (equity) in the project. You probably won't be able to borrow money without showing that you carry some risk yourself.

Expect to put up around 30 percent of the cost to develop residential property yourself. For big-ticket items like shopping malls or industrial parks, your equity could be less — depending on how many investors are involved, what kind of security you offer, and your financial strength. If you already own other property, you can use that as collateral for a new loan.

The most likely sticking point for the lender is going to be whether you'll be working at the right level, considering your resources and ability. If you've managed large projects in the past, then qualification won't be an issue. But if you've only been in business for a year or two, and you've never tried land development before, you should start small.

Housing Options

As we've said, lenders are often most familiar with financing single-family homes, so they're comfortable evaluating requests from developers for financing those types of subdivisions. Don't assume that your bank's loan committee knows about less-common housing types. You may want to look for larger lenders with specialized loan departments if your development plans include condos, multifamily units or vacation housing.

Condominiums

Condominium and co-op developments can present special problems for loan officers. They're aware that these involve a corporate approach to ownership, including provisions in the purchase contract that restricts not only what owners may do with their properties, but might even require preapproval of new buyers by existing association members. Some lenders are put off by the covenants, conditions, and restrictions, even though those don't really affect financing for the developer.

Lenders may be more receptive to financing projects involving conversion of apartment units to condos and co-ops, because they understand that conversion means that a converted condominium buyer pays the developer when they buy the unit. The lender sees that as making a loan less risky.

You might be asked to let the lender's legal department review your covenant documents which describe conditions attached to the units that restrict how buyers can use or alter the property. The lender may even propose changes to the covenant documents as a condition of your loan.

Rental Units

Lenders understand apartment developments better than they do cooperative units. But here, a different problem comes up. It's harder to analyze demand for apartments than for single-family homes, because it fluctuates more quickly and over a wider range. For example, when a college or university dominates a town, apartment demand might fall off dramatically during the summer break.

Your loan officer realizes that it's easier for tenants to move than it is for homeowners, so they may be spooked by the prospect of high vacancy rates. That will be less of a problem for you if you plan to sell all the units at once to a single buyer instead of renting them out yourself.

You may still have to demonstrate to your lender how your cash flow projections are prepared to manage worst-case scenarios — cases where demand falls off and occupancy rates drop. Lenders may require that you anticipate a 10 to 20 percent vacancy factor, even when there's no historical reason to expect such levels.

Retirement Housing

These developments may include amenities like common areas, a club house, and recreation facilities. Some complexes offer assisted living, including housekeeping, meal services and medical care. You'll need to prove to your lender that you thoroughly understand that market and have considered the specialized features that make these developments attractive.

Vacation Homes

Coastal regions, lakes, mountain ski resorts, hunting and fishing areas, and entertainment centers are where people look for a second home. But you'll find that lenders are reluctant to finance projects in what is historically a soft market. In too many vacation home developments, initial appeals lead to few solid sales, and many units end up unsold. Defaults by buyers are also higher than for primary residences.

Lenders are particularly cautious about time-share developments where there's been virtually no secondary market in the past. Once people buy their shares, they're stuck with them.

Your market study has to be especially convincing for you to prove that your project will sell well, instead of leaving the lender holding the bag. If you can't support your argument that qualified buyers will be attracted to your development, it might be a blessing to be turned down. If your idea is truly a good one, your research will make your point, and a lender will agree with you.

Planned Communities

Modern suburbs are characterized by carefully-planned communities which develop in predictable patterns because they've been defined down to the smallest detail before even grading begins or a single foundation is poured. In some places, local regulations require that development can't occur unless there's a master plan. The developer (usually with help from consultants) writes the master plan, which specifies all design, environmental, and aesthetic elements of the development, including:

▌ Street and lot layout, including control of traffic patterns within the community, and access to arterial roads and freeways.

▌ Materials to be used in construction. Even though local building codes specify the quality of materials, some design decisions and cosmetic issues are controlled by the master plan. For example, a planned community, much like a condo or co-op development, may restrict outside paint colors beyond the four or five "acceptable" colors agreed to in advance. A neighborhood or community covenant may also specify exterior materials, preventing owners from later applying certain types of siding or roofing.

▌ Building style. Here's where some people object to planned communities. They feel the tight restrictions produce a kind of sterility and lack of imagination. But lenders like them because there's no uncertainty about zoning, approvals from planners, or other troubling matters that can kill a project. If your development is part of a larger plan, cite that plan when you take your project to the lender.

▌ Location of all structures. The plan (or the zoning regulations) may specify not only lot sizes, but where structures can be built on those lots. Some plans plat out lots so that structures are clustered. This forces density into a relatively small area and leaves the rest of the tract as open space.

Figure 3-1 shows how such clustering typically works. In the illustration, each large box is five acres. The black squares represent structures. Roads run to the left and right of this four-lot square, with driveway access close to the lot lines. That leaves the greater part of all four lots vacant.

▌ Specifications for all utilities.

▌ Open space, including designated parks, landscaping and buffer zones.

The plan also covers all these planning issues:

▌ Grading, drainage and stability.

▌ Zoning and density limitations. The community plan normally specifies maximum density. You can't exceed that density, and once it's reached, the land can't be further subdivided. Of course, you can have fewer dwelling units than the plan allows. For example, in Figure 3-1, a person could buy two or more sections and consolidate them, then build only one house in the middle that would be surrounded by up to $19\frac{1}{2}$ acres of open space!

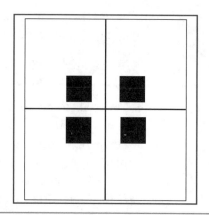

Figure 3-1 Typical clustered housing plan

▌ Location with respect to existing residential, commercial and industrial centers.

▌ Access to existing transportation corridors.

▌ Proximity to required services such as police and fire protection, schools, churches, recreational areas, and shops.

▌ Target market. This doesn't mean the planners decide who can live there. But it does dictate to some extent who can afford to live there. A planned community can be designed to offer executive-style homes, affordable housing, family homes, "empty nest" dwellings, bachelor pads, or any combination of these. Either way, they're built for a target market. No planner will tread on the dangerous ground of discrimination by being specific about the kind of people they want to attract. But economic forces and the design of the project itself determine the target market.

▌ Conformance to regional plans, where applicable.

▌ Environmental review.

Many of the issues that are important to people concerned about growth (like density restrictions, neighborhood schools, designated open space and traffic management) are usually covered in master plans. Growth opponents are often placated when they're included in the master planning process, where they can negotiate concessions within the plan.

The master plan provides a way to lock in assurances between the developer and the community. A well-designed plan helps them both win; the community gets a quality project and the developer makes a profit.

If you plan to approach your city or county planning department with an idea for a planned community development yourself, you'll need to hire an experienced land use consultant and be prepared to face a huge management task. Procedures vary from place to place, but you're sure to face a dizzying number of requirements imposed by local government agencies.

Remember, you'll be developing an entire self-contained community, and that includes housing, commercial areas, schools, churches, public service facilities and perhaps even government offices. In a case like this, one group often coordinates the whole project as general contractor or joint venture leader. Or the city or county might control the project, while developers buy up segments of the land and invite contractors to bid on parts of the development.

Developing one of those parts of a planned community can affect your profit, too. Zoning and services are probably already in place by the time you purchase building lots, so they'll be more expensive than starting with cheaper raw land. But you won't face the expense and uncertainty of providing services to a remote area.

Nonresidential Development

We define the two major kinds of development as residential and nonresidential. Nonresidential development includes commercial and industrial projects, which are defined by the amount of contact between workers and the general public. Commercial development employs office workers, salespeople or service providers who deal with clients or customers. This includes professionals like doctors, dentists or attorneys, and other self-employed people who offer services rather than products. Industrial employers hire manufacturing workers or equipment operators who have little, if any, contact with the public.

Here's a more detailed breakdown:

1. Commercial

   ▌ Retail

   ▌ Hotel and motel

   ▌ Office and office park

   ▌ Healthcare, including resident care facilities

   ▌ Recreational uses, including theaters, bowling or fitness centers and gyms, camping and RV parks

   ▌ Private schools, daycare centers

2. Industrial

   ▌ Light-impact industrial, which includes warehousing, light manufacturing, storage, or rail-to-truck freight exchange

   ▌ Heavy-impact industrial

Whether a development is light- or heavy-impact industrial depends on how severely it affects nearby land uses.

We mentioned earlier that bankers are more comfortable with single-family-housing loans than with other residential developments. Lenders are even less familiar, and also less comfortable, with nonresidential developments. You have to educate them, or else look for a lender that employs experts in the nonresidential market.

Your market study helps you with this because it provides lenders with economic facts that address their concerns about risk. You can argue that:

▌ The local land supply inventory figures might be inflated because not all land designated for your kind of development is available for that use.

▌ Land will be more valuable following a rezone to a use that's in high demand.

▌ Demand also increases the market value of improvements.

▌ Past trends predict future growth in the market for your project.

Points like this help show that your nonresidential plan will succeed in response to demand.

You'll approach a lender differently, depending on your project's type of land use. The greater the impact of a particular project, the more restrictions you may face before you can develop the land. You may have to justify:

▌ Responses to environmental impact, including mitigation activities

▌ Location of the project as related to other land uses

From the lender's point of view, these translate into more uncertainty because of greater expense and longer development time. And, as we've said before, lenders don't like uncertainties.

You might have to pay for environmental studies. Some of your land may be lost to buffers or habitat protection. You could even have to defend your plan in court if a well-funded no-growth group decides to block you. They may appeal after your zoning request is granted. That's a common way opponents delay projects, hoping that the developer will run out of money (and patience) and scuttle the plan rather than fight the appeals to get final approval. Time is on their side, not yours.

You'll need to be sure your development plan is thorough and accurate. Know up front what objections your project may raise. But no matter how thorough you are, that still might not be enough. Be sure you can prove to the lender that their doubts and uncertainty about your project aren't justified — that you've anticipated and paved the way to overcome any hurdles thrown in your way by opposition to your project.

Commercial Development

The following trends appear in the national market for commercial development:

▌ New office development occurs in the suburbs rather than in city cores. This is especially the case where the trend is for sprawling lower-height buildings with their own parking lots, or security garages instead of more traditional inner-city high-rises. Space limitations in the city core, cheaper land (and perhaps lower taxes) in outlying areas, and often shorter commutes for employees, are making suburban planned commercial developments attractive to developers and businesses alike.

▌ Demand for office development is expected to decline dramatically by 2010, as more and more people work from home and communicate over the Internet. For example, insurance claims offices employ many people and have used a lot of office space in the past. Now they're hiring people to do the work on their home computers and transmit results by fax, e-mail or FTP.

▌ In the past 25 years, the amount of retail space in the U.S. has tripled. Retail development seems to have peaked during the 1990s. While small mall development has been popular in the past, trends show that now the market is getting soft. This means you should be very careful about selecting such projects.

Statistics represent estimates of national averages, but supply and demand vary greatly from place to place. Demand for retail space may boom in some areas and lag in others. For example, development sites in areas near the Canadian or Mexican borders could be either excellent or poor locations, depending on trends in international exchange rates.

▌ Today, discount centers and warehouse clubs compete for business with malls, and catalog shopping (including the Internet) may further reduce retail space requirements for the future. This trend is likely to continue, especially in planned community developments where local shopping centers replace traditional downtown shopping areas. Identify your market carefully for commercial development to see how your ideas will fit in with changes in ways that people shop.

▌ Electronic shopping, which in the late 1990s accounted for less than 10 percent of the retail market, could be the big growth area in retail's future. This emerging trend may be too new to reliably predict future conditions. But for developers, retail is probably the one area posing the greatest future uncertainty.

▌ With the aging of the population, the demand for health care facilities — medical offices, retirement and convalescent homes — will continue to increase. The unique features of such facilities will probably lead to a specialized development market in the future. If your area has a higher-than-average concentration of retired people, health care facilities will certainly be a big market in future development.

You can see that many of the statistical studies seem to indicate a slowing of past trends. That doesn't always mean that demand for a particular form of development will go away. It's only a sign that the demand is leveling off.

Remember that national trends are useful only to indicate an overall direction. Local trends are the only ones that really count when you make your plans. In extreme cases, even a distance of 20 miles or less can cause a sizable difference in economic and political climates. Neighboring counties can have widely varying points of view about growth. Employers may feel welcome in one town and be rejected a few miles away.

There are things you can look for locally that will dispute trends in the national averages:

▌ A big warehouse sales company opens up in your town, but soon closes down. The same thing happens to a large retail store. You see that local people prefer smaller, more service-oriented shops, and the big impersonal concept just doesn't work where you live. A cluster of specialty shops would probably be more attractive to residents.

▌ You live near the Canadian border and, while the Canadian dollar has been weak for many years, you see recent changes in that trend. It might indicate that Canadian shoppers will be more eager to cross the border to shop.

▌ Local political leadership has changed recently and an anti-growth trend has suddenly reversed. A new planning director has pledged to encourage relocation of light-impact manufacturing firms and new commercial interests. This points to a likely increased demand for development in the future.

Industrial Development

As much as commercial development might worry some loan officers, industrial projects are even more troublesome. The market for industrial development is perplexing, at best. In some industries, demand is at an all-time high. For example, multimodal facilities (where freight is transferred between ships, trains and trucks) are popular, especially where volume is high and heavy truck traffic is ruining the local freeways. These centers can help divert tons of materials away from the interstates and onto the railroads or waterways for long hauls.

Likewise, light manufacturing and just-in-time delivery facilities appeal to distributors in strategically-located regions, especially in border and port cities. These centers provide warehousing for components where parts can be held for delivery to their final destinations where and when they're needed. Manufacturers at both ends of the pipeline save money and space required to maintain large inventories.

It's still too early to judge the long-term effects of the North American Free Trade Agreement (NAFTA), but the exchange of goods between the U.S., Mexico and Canada may significantly affect where and how industrial development occurs. Investors currently favor multimodal and warehousing developments as sources for the highest returns. This is particularly true in border areas and along connecting interstate highway and rail routes.

Getting financing for industrial projects may be hard if your lender doesn't understand this market. Trends are confusing because many sub-markets exist within the market for industrial development. The sub-markets include warehousing, shipping, component manufacturing, distribution, customs brokerages, container storage, train marshaling, and storage yards. These lead to related support services such as offices, truck stops, fuel and maintenance stations, and food service.

Here are examples of confusing statistics:

▌ From 1980 to 1995, national average manufacturing output grew at more than 2 percent per year, while national average manufacturing employment fell by more than 0.5 percent per year.

▌ In the same period, productivity grew by an average of nearly 3 percent per year while construction grew by less than 0.5 percent.

To loan officers (and to many contractors, estimators, architects and engineers), there's always been a direct relationship between output and employment. There's also been the same connection between productivity and the construction of manufacturing sites.

So what's going on? The answer is that the manufacturing industry has changed.

▌ U.S. manufacturing companies spend more today on research and development at home, while moving manufacturing operations to other countries. That's because of relaxed international tariff rules combined with lower labor costs overseas.

▌ Productivity has improved in recent years. Today, the typical worker produces 60 percent more goods per hour than in 1980.

Your role as an educator becomes even more important when you approach a lender for an industrial project. Anticipate their questions. Be prepared to demonstrate that you're aware of recent changes in the industrial and manufacturing sectors and explain why your project answers the needs of the current market.

Master Plans for Nonresidential Uses

The master plan is most often associated with housing development. But planners will happily consider a master plan for commercial and industrial development as well. Planners love to engineer everything about the way we live — including where we work and play — and how we travel from one place to another. So before you can get financing, you'll need to know (among other things) that you can get the necessary permits, and that your project will pass environmental review. For that to happen, you'll have to fulfill the planning department's requirements and demands. A master plan which includes consideration for open space, habitat, and compatibility with nearby land use is a useful tool for doing that.

Without a master plan, developers use only the land they already own, excluding nearby property owners. When a development proves successful, owners of small nearby lots want to cash in on the opportunities. Not only is there money to be made, but development sometimes means that surrounding land uses don't work anymore. Your chicken farm or salvage yard probably won't make much sense if a financial center opens up next door!

Owners of small parcels must decide whether to hold out and continue using their property as they always have, sell out to the developer, or become a minority partner in the development project. Often they actually have little choice; their hand is forced by financial pressure, or by conditions dictated by the planning department, where a master plan prevents piecemeal development.

The master plan is especially appropriate when a relatively large area targeted for development has several different owners. Zoning changes will prevent island pockets of incompatible use designations. The master plan might be the only practical way for all the owners to work together for their mutual benefit. It prevents piecemeal development and gives the relatively smaller parcel owners a chance to profitably develop their properties.

A master-plan developer can deal with smaller property owners in several ways:

▌ Buy their land outright.

▌ Get options to buy the land and development rights in exchange for a fixed payment or the promise of equity sharing when the project is sold.

▌ Share costs for services and improvements with other owners on a per-acre-owned basis.

Example: A community wanted to develop a 200-acre area as a major industrial site. It included a major rail line and spur, and was close to a major freeway. The property was far away from existing or planned housing. The county had already designated the area in its comprehensive plan as an industrial site, subject to development of a master plan approved by a majority of the 15 property owners.

All the owners depended upon one another for different reasons. The developer created a plan which solved two major problems:

▌ Some owners of smaller parcels on the borders of the development area were afraid that their lots couldn't be developed, since they provide sight and noise buffers for interior properties.

▌ The owners of the interior properties wanted the right to access the railroad spur as part of a larger plan.

Without a master plan, the alternative would be for planners to review a series of permit requests from individual owners over time. That could result in poorly-organized, piecemeal development. The master plan was a sensible compromise because it provided basic services, and it spread assessments fairly between property owners.

Most of the owners agreed to the terms of the master plan, which distributed improvement costs by the acre. But some owners were against the whole plan and didn't want to pay for their share of developing a master plan, for assessments to run utilities and improve roads for the entire area, or for any other costs not related to their own land.

To account for the holdouts, the plan spelled out how a latecomer's fee schedule would work. As a result, the property owners (except the original holdouts) eventually participated in paying to prepare the master plan. Most of the small-property owners sold their lots, and the master plan was executed by the company that eventually owned about three-fourths of all the land.

During the master plan negotiations with the property owners, the developer financed the whole development (with the lender's help). This arrangement is possible only if and when the developer, with a majority of the owners, can proceed with the all-important approval of the planning department. Remember, approval of the master plan is only one requirement.

The developer also needs other participants to go along. In many cases, the owners approve of the idea but can't — or won't — pay their share.

Owners participating with the developer did so willingly and had to pay the part of the expenses that opponents didn't want to pay. Those owners who held out had to pay the latecomer's fee when they sold their appreciated property at fully-serviced industrial prices. The latecomer's fee is designed to cover the additional interest costs the developer had to absorb.

Outright purchase is the least appealing to developers, who usually prefer to offer future benefits over current payment.

In a typical case, several owners cooperate in designing a master plan. The plan goes before the planning department as the first step toward getting the necessary permits. When you enter into a master-planned development with other owners, either you own part of the property already, or you have options to buy from one or more current owners. Usually the developer who owns most of the land drives the project.

The lender won't approve your project unless you have some equity in the development — either by owning at least part of the land outright, or by already having financing for your part of land in an area involving other owners.

The master plan puts order into the development process when more than one owner is involved.

Often, the kind of work involving latecomer's fees include things like road widening, running of utilities, and construction of higher-capacity water towers. They're things that don't intrude on someone's land, but benefit them by adding value to that land.

The master plan works just as well for any development that requires consolidation of properties, like a large shopping area or mall. It also applies to a mixed-use area combining retail and residential zoning, or to developments with several zoning designations so that related businesses or services are close to one another.

Property Management

Sometimes the market turns sour and you're forced to rent or lease your development because you can't sell it. But an alternative is to develop property with the intention of holding it for future gain. In this case, your goal is to arrange long-term financing so you can lease the finished space, get the cash flow started, and give the land and improvements some time to season. During the course of this process, you change from a developer into a land manager and landlord. Of course, if that's not the role you want to play, you can subcontract out those activities and move on to a new development project.

This type of project requires what lenders refer to as "permanent" financing. It isn't really permanent, because lenders always want their money back (with interest) eventually. But the term could extend 20 or 30 years instead of 20 or 30 months.

The problem with this is that lenders are hesitant to grant long-term loans for development, particularly to a novice developer. They want to see a proven track record before they'll take the risk. You'd be better off to apply for short-term financing with the idea of selling the project when it's finished.

Then you can change your plans later if everything goes well. You can go back to the lender, showing that you made your payments on time, finished the project on schedule and within your budget — and that you can show a positive cash flow from a fully-rented project. At that stage, they're more likely to consider long-term financing because few things are more convincing to a lender than past success.

You can see that there are many possible routes into land development. All types of development share certain characteristics:

▌ They each have a unique market.

▌ Their potential for success follows the rules of supply and demand.

▌ They all take money to turn plans into reality.

It's important to choose your development path carefully.

Sometimes the markets for different types of development have little to do with each other. And while their cycles are certainly related, their timing may be very different. Residential development might be booming to keep pace with demand at the same time that commercial or industrial facilities stand vacant because they were overbuilt earlier.

All this explains why it's important to choose your development path carefully. If conditions aren't good for one type of development, they may be excellent for another. Analyze all your options before you go on. Study the statistics and trends, then look at all the markets to decide which way you want to proceed. Perhaps the best early decision you can make is to proceed slowly.

Chapter 4

Find the *Right* Land

Your land market study showed you what's available. You've reviewed your development choices with that in mind. Now it's time to target the best property for your project.

After all, the site itself has a lot to do with the success of your development. Consider its geographic location, zoning, available services, surrounding land uses and anticipated growth patterns. They'll all affect its suitability now and its potential for increased value later.

Your land analysis from Chapter 2 reveals answers to these questions about the available land:

▌ Are there suitable lots available in your area?

▌ Which parcels are of an appropriate size?

▌ Which (if any) are already zoned for your preferred use, or have the best prospects for rezoning?

▌ Which services and amenities are already in place?

Now it's time for you to narrow your field of choices. You have to gather more information before you can answer these three questions:

1. Which parcel is the best buy, considering the readiness of the land for development?

2. Which characteristics of each property make it more (or less) suitable for my project?

3. Can I provide all the improvements necessary to produce my development and still make money?

A lender probably won't consider your application unless your development plan is based on a specific piece of land. If your company is in excellent financial shape and you have a good credit history, you *might* get pre-approval. But final approval will depend on your project plan, which includes the physical features and profit potential of the land you choose to develop.

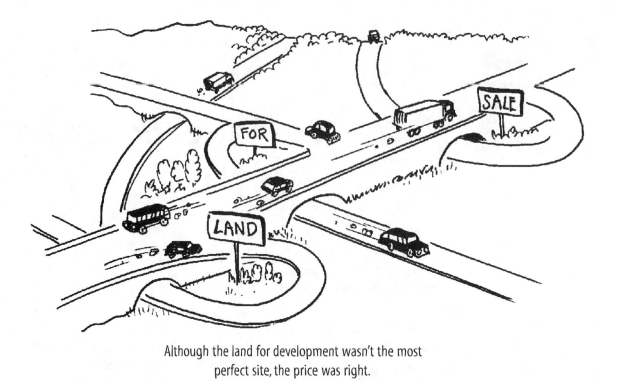

Although the land for development wasn't the most
perfect site, the price was right.

Your land inventory probably covered two kinds of development sites: raw land and improved land. Raw land lacks most, if not all, basic services such as roads, gas, electricity, water, telephone, sewer, refuse collection, or storm drains. Improved land may have some or all of these. You'll have to provide (or be assessed for) some or all of the others, plus in some cases, cable for TV and Internet service.

The more services there are already in place, the more the land costs to buy. The previous owner paid for utilities and infrastructure through ULIDs (Utility Local Improvement Districts), which assess costs through special taxes and fees added to property tax bills. And they'll pass those costs on to you.

In some cases, basic services will be "available," but not yet installed. That means that plans are already in place to run those services to the land, in which case you face one of two prospects. Either:

1. The basic services have not yet been paid for and you, as new owner, will be assessed for all or part of the cost. (You can probably finance such assessments over a period of years, with interest.)

2. A previous owner already paid up front for the services, and their cost is included in the price of the land.

One way or another, you're paying for basic services.

A Checklist for Site Selection

Your lender or investor will want to know why you chose *that* land over another parcel somewhere else. You can propose more than one potential site, but show why you favor one over the other(s). Let's consider some ways to learn about and evaluate available sites.

The perfect piece of ground for your development will be:

Location.
Land characteristics.
Environmental conditions.
Improvements.
Zoning issues.
Price.

▌ Affordable

▌ Flat

▌ Dry

▌ Conveniently located adjacent to town and in the "path of progress"

▌ Zoned properly or a good target for rezoning

▌ Close to transportation corridors

▌ A safe distance from the nearest earthquake fault or flood channel

▌ Improved to provide basic services

▌ Free of endangered insects, birds, animals or plant life

If you've found a parcel like that, you don't need to go through the steps in the rest of this chapter. Just plan the job, get your money, and start building. But it's more likely that your land options are somewhat less than perfect. You have to compare the sites, then pick the one that gives you the best shot at a profitable project.

Figure 4-1 lists many of the topics you'll need to cover when you narrow your choice of sites. The type of information you gather will be the same whether your project is residential, commercial, or industrial, but you may apply it differently.

You can find some of the information by looking at a road map, a topographic map, or a geologic survey of the area. Your city or county planning or engineering departments may have information about water tables, percolation rates, and soil characteristics. Or you may have to hire a soils engineer to get this information for you.

You can find data about vehicle trips through:

▌ Local transportation agencies affiliated with your county

▌ The state government transportation agency

▌ The U.S. Department of Transportation

Land characteristics

Define in terms of grading and excavation, foundation requirements.

❏ Soil type: Is it sandy, rocky, full of clay?

❏ Vegetation: Are there trees you can incorporate as a noise or sight buffer, or as an open space corridor for common use? Or will you clear everything to provide landscape?

❏ Water table, percolation rate: Will these affect foundations and drainage?

❏ Flood plane: Near enough to provide a hazard?

❏ Elevations: Is the property level? Hilly? Marked by canyons? Are there rock formations that will hamper grading?

❏ Earthquake faults: How close and how risky?

❏ Water: Lakes, lagoons, rivers, streams or ponds?

❏ Other _____

Services

Check those already in place. If not, how much will it cost to provide them, if required?

❏ Water _____

❏ Gas _____

❏ Electricity _____

❏ Telephone _____

❏ Cable _____

❏ Sewers, storm drains _____

❏ Trash disposal _____

❏ Other _____

Improvements

❏ How much will it cost to install services and improvements?

❏ What will I have to build?

❏ What will I be assessed for?

❏ Power lines or transmission towers: Where are they? Will they interfere with my plans?

❏ Roads: Location? Are they adequate to handle increased traffic generated by my project?

❏ Traffic loads on major streets and highways?

❏ Existing buildings: Will I need to demolish them?

❏ Transportation infrastructure: Proximity of railroad lines, ports, freeways?

❏ Other _____

Figure 4-1 Parcel evaluation

Amenities

Which of the following are conveniently located or accessible?
- ❏ Grade school
- ❏ Middle school
- ❏ High school
- ❏ Fire protection
- ❏ Law enforcement

Zoning issues

- ❏ Is the property already annexed to the local zoning jurisdiction?
- ❏ If not, is assurance forthcoming that it will be?
- ❏ How is the parcel zoned now?
- ❏ How has the parcel been used in the past?
- ❏ How are nearby or adjacent plots zoned?
- ❏ Are nearby zonings compatible?
- ❏ Local regulatory climate and prospects for rezone?
- ❏ Other _____

Location

- ❏ Is this parcel clearly in the path of progress?
- ❏ Relationship of site to nearby and adjacent properties.
- ❏ Access to existing services and amenities.
- ❏ Distance to shopping, entertainment, recreation.
- ❏ Distance from "undesirable" uses: Trash processing, heavy industrial, etc.
- ❏ Access to transportation links: Freeways, commuter rail, shipping hubs.
- ❏ Special benefits of this location for my project.

Price

- ❏ Raw land: Will the added cost of improvements exceed our budgeted land cost per building unit?
- ❏ Improved land: Is the increased cost adequately offset by existing improvements?

Environmental conditions

- ❏ Protected wetlands
- ❏ Host to endangered habitat
- ❏ Nearby hazards, natural and man-made
- ❏ Noise levels (existing and resulting from improvements)
- ❏ Percentage of useable land (not restricted by mitigation)
- ❏ Other _____

Figure 4-1 Parcel evaluation (continued)

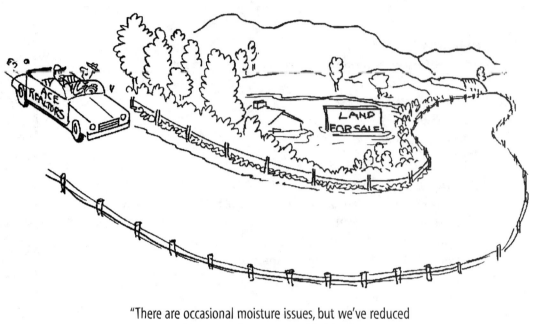

"There are occasional moisture issues, but we've reduced the price a bit to account for that."

Of special interest to industrial sites will be truck volume, so be sure to check weigh station statistics. Track these over time to spot a trend and predict future conditions. Weigh station numbers demonstrate not only the volume of truck traffic through an area, but also the trend. How do today's traffic volumes compare with those of last year? Five years ago? Are they staying the same or growing? In developing an industrial site, weigh station trends point to likely future volume. For example, if a particular area is experiencing a lot of residential growth, that translates to greater need for commercial and industrial support facilities — if not today, then in the future. Increases in truck traffic often foretell what's going to be happening next year and the year after.

Environmental agencies can furnish information about habitats, protected lands, environmental restrictions, setbacks, and mitigation requirements.

Will you need to demolish existing improvements, or are they useful to you in some way? Can they be incorporated into your plans? For instance, perhaps an existing home or business can generate rental income during your financing and planning phases, before you have to tear it down to make way for new construction.

All these issues influence how practical your plan will be, and whether your project will make a good profit. Your lender or investor will want to know that you've investigated them all thoroughly, so you won't encounter unwelcome surprises down the line.

Feasibility Analysis

Location_____Date_____

Street Address _____

City_____

Land Costs

Land purchase price _____
Land closing costs _____
Off-site improvement _____
Demolition & clearing _____
On-site improvement _____
   Total land costs _____

Development Costs

Survey & topo maps _____
Percolation test _____
Architectural & design services _____
Engineering fees _____
Soil testing _____
Environment testing _____
Plan copies & reprints _____
Market & feasibility studies _____
Appraisal fees _____
Insurance _____
Property taxes _____
Legal & accounting _____
Building permits & fees _____
Utility fees _____
Administrative overhead _____
Interest reserve _____
   Total development costs _____

Financing Costs

Interest on land _____
Land development _____
Construction loan fees _____
Construction loan closing costs _____
Construction loan interest _____
   Total financing costs _____

Construction Costs

Total construction cost _____
Total land cost _____
Total development cost _____
Total finance cost _____
Total construction cost _____
   Subtotal project costs _____

Marketing & Closing Costs

Sales commissions _____
Advertising _____
Closing costs _____
Other costs paid by seller _____
   Total marketing & closing costs _____

Total Project Cost Summary

Land cost _____
Development cost _____
Financing cost _____
Construction cost _____
Marketing & closing costs _____
   Total project costs _____

Analysis Summary

Estimated sales price _____
Total project cost (subtotal) _____
Net profit _____

Figure 4-2 Feasibility analysis

For each promising plot you found in your land analysis, you'll need more information to make the cut to the best possible one. You can use the feasibility analysis in Figure 4-2 to help you decide among them. You'll need all this information before you can do the takeoffs and estimates for your business plan — and before you can convince a lender or investor that your development plan will make money for you both.

Land Use Consultants

If you have trouble finding out about the land or interpreting local zoning ordinances, consider hiring a land use consultant or attorney to help you avoid a bad buy. That person can also help you get zoning changes, conditional-use permits and building permits.

To find a qualified land use consultant, don't just depend on the Yellow Pages. Ask other developers to recommend people. Go to public meetings where land use issues are discussed. Chances are you'll see consultants in action and have a chance to meet them.

These people often have engineering or planning backgrounds. They should understand land use laws, environmental issues and local politics. Find someone who has experience in your type of project, who listens well, explains things clearly, and will work with you to make sure you find the best possible site for your project.

You might be able to get by without hiring high-priced land consultants, but good ones can steer you through the political and bureaucratic maze, as well as help you to prepare your case well for the local review process. Many developers are faced with a staggering number of requirements: environmental impact reports, master plans, political struggles on the local level, competing interests with similar projects, anti-growth sentiment — all adding up to problems and potential rejection of your development ideas. If you're facing problems like these, a land use consultant who's knowledgeable in both legal requirements and the political climate can be a life saver.

Chapter 5

Alternatives to Borrowing

You've found the perfect piece of property for your project and you're confident your plan will make money. But you don't have enough cash to buy the lot. What next? Before you go running off to the local building & loan, consider this: *Maybe you don't have to borrow right away — and perhaps not at all!*

The secret is to use *OPM* (other people's money) as long as you can.

You'll face some hurdles before you can acquire the property, no matter how you finance the land. For example, if the land hasn't been platted yet, you might need to apply for a plat approval and wait until any appeal periods have expired before any lender will commit to a loan.

The platting process officially identifies property boundaries and locations of any improvements. Platting doesn't involve environmental review or zoning. Those are separate steps that can make your project more complicated — which also means it will probably take longer to complete.

The appeal period for a plat map usually runs about 30 days. This gives other property owners a chance to register their objections to the tract layout, and for state or federal agencies to protest if they believe any undue impacts will result from the project. It's common for environmental concerns to be raised at this point. Even though filing a plat map itself has no effect on the environment, agencies may appeal based on their concerns that platting is the first step to more harmful actions later.

There are three ways you can secure your building site without first having your loan approved:

▌ Work directly with the seller

▌ Use options (or buy a right of first refusal)

▌ Arrange a 1031 exchange

These are all ways to get a commitment from the owner to sell you the property with little or no cash up front. We'll discuss the variations of each method.

Dave understood well the concept of using OPM (Other People's Money)
to finance his project, but may have misunderstood the
book's suggestions for getting it.

Work Directly With the Seller

I'll begin by saying that when a seller has an active listing with a real estate agent, you must work through that agent. Any attempt to deal directly with a seller who's under contract with a real estate agent could get you *and* the seller into legal trouble. The agent will likely sue the seller for any commissions due if you attempt to make a deal behind the agent's back.

It's OK to approach a landowner whose listing with an agent has expired. But be cautious. Even in this case, a real estate agent might try to make a case for collecting a commission. They could argue that their advertising of the property brought the buyer to the table. That may be hard for them to prove, but they may be willing to give it a try. If they do, whether you win or lose, you still probably lose. Few people other than the lawyers come out ahead in court. Better be on the safe side and approach sellers carefully after a listing has expired. Don't go banging on their door the day after the "For Sale" sign comes down.

It's true that developers have more of a bargaining advantage in a buyer's market where there's plenty of land available and prices are low. But even when land is at a premium, you may be able to negotiate more favorable terms by working directly with an owner rather than through a conventional lender.

Sellers often believe that they can get a better price for their property if they carry the loan themselves. Here are some reasons for that:

▌ Buyers may have qualification problems. Maybe you can't qualify for a mortgage loan for the property. If the seller is willing to carry the loan, you'll be less concerned with price and more anxious about just making the deal.

▌ Seller's negotiating power. When the seller carries the mortgage, they're in a good position to ask a higher price to offset their risk. A full-price offer on the buyer's part will probably be part of the mix.

▌ Greater after-tax profit. The seller spreads profits over several years using the installment sale method to report capital gains. Payments over several years spread the tax burden over several years, which may keep the seller's tax bracket lower as well.

Even though the benefits seem stacked in favor of the seller, you may be able to negotiate some favorable terms, including:

▌ Low (or no) down payment

▌ Reduced interest

▌ Payments postponed until the project is finished

Become a partner with the owner.

Your biggest challenge here is to show the landowner (and the owner's attorney) that both you and the seller benefit by working together. You become partners with the property owner in *spirit*, if not in fact. You both need to be confident that the deal will work out to everyone's advantage.

It might be hard to convince the seller to let you buy the land with no money down. The owner's risk goes up as your down payment goes down. When you have no equity interest in the property, sellers may think it's easy for you to just walk away from the deal. They believe that money up front motivates buyers to work out problems. But no-down-payment deals mean less of your cash is tied up in the property at the outset, even though you'll make higher payments and pay more interest down the line.

You can argue that this also benefits the seller. They get more money and earn more interest each month. You can also use this to induce a seller who owns property free and clear to provide financing by offering an attractive interest rate.

You might be able to persuade a seller who occupies their property to finance the purchase if you offer them an attractive rental agreement from the time you close the deal until you begin construction. But be sure to put the agreement in writing, and specify the date by which they must vacate the property. You don't want to forget this.

Contingencies

Whether you work directly with the seller or through a lender, your deal will probably involve contingencies — they're part of normal business. And many transactions fall through because the contingencies aren't met. That's why they're covered in the contract. No one should commit to a real estate deal without fully understanding the contingencies that define the contract, including things like getting construction loans or zoning changes.

These elements make up a contingency agreement:

▌ The sales contract

▌ Tangible evidence (money!) of the buyer's serious intent

▌ The receipt documenting feasibility and contingency clauses

We'll begin with the last one. The purpose of the receipt isn't to prove that money (or a note) changed hands, but rather to document the feasibility clause and special contingencies. *It must be in writing to be binding.* Both the buyer and seller must sign the receipt and receive a copy. Local rules vary, so you need to be sure that the language is appropriate for the laws in your area.

The importance of contingencies.

The contingency clause is critical because it guarantees that you can walk away from the deal without penalty or liability if it turns out that the project isn't feasible.

In Chapter 9 we discuss *technical* feasibility as a marketing and financial issue. That's a different matter. To be feasible, as we use the term here, your plan has to make sense and be workable, or the whole deal will fall through. You can't always know whether a plan is feasible until you begin the steps to actually buy the land. Here are some things that could prove your plan *isn't* feasible:

▌ Environmental review determines that the land is habitat for a protected or endangered species and can't be developed.

▌ Planners deny your application for a required zoning change.

▌ Soils engineers discover toxic or dangerous conditions on or in the land.

▌ You find that the land is prone to flooding.

▌ Growth opponents stage a well-organized opposition, including threatened lawsuits, that's too overwhelming to beat.

The receipt isn't the real estate contract itself, but it does spell out the conditions that go into developing the contract. It's actually an amendment to the real estate contract, like any other additions or changes. The contract itself contains basic provisions — standard contract language, identification of the parties, location of the property, selling price, terms of payment, and standard contingencies.

The receipt should include:

- The names and addresses of both parties

- A description of the land, which includes the number of acres involved, the address and abbreviated legal description, and plat numbers if available

- A brief description of your development project

- A deadline to determine feasibility

- A statement that you, the potential buyer, have the final word on feasibility

- Your promise to begin resolving the contingencies immediately

Most contingencies have to do with planning issues. For example, you need a cooperative seller if you have to get plat approval. The seller must be willing to agree that the sale is contingent upon plat approval and a commitment from a lender or investor to finance the project.

You might want a clause specifying that you'll be reimbursed for specific expenses if the sellers don't perform an agreed-upon step (such as removing trash from the property), or if they take some action that hampers your progress.

There's one risk you can't protect against with a contingency clause. That's when a deal falls apart through no fault on the part of either you or the seller. In that case, you're out the cost of any work you've done, even if it adds value to the seller's property.

The seller might want some contingencies of their own. But here are some examples of contingencies you probably *wouldn't* want to accept from the seller:

- The deal won't close until the seller finds a new residence or business location. This is a common contingency requested by sellers. But it wouldn't be reasonable because you'll be working against deadlines. You need to know *exactly* when the seller will vacate the property.

- The seller might want the option to keep some part of the land. This would interfere with your development plans if the plans depend on having the entire plot available.

Earnest Money Options

The purpose of earnest money is to protect the seller by making sure you don't just walk away from the deal without a good reason — one that's specified in the contingencies of the real estate contract. Be sure your real estate contract specifies what will happen to the earnest money deposit or note in case the sale, and project, fall through. You should be entitled to cancellation without penalty if it turns out that your plan isn't feasible.

The amount of the earnest money deposit depends largely on the price of the land and should reflect the value of the deal. "Standard" deposits vary by region and type of property. But in any case, the more you offer, the more sincere you appear as a buyer.

You may need to pledge or deposit more if your deal contains many contingencies that may be hard to satisfy. But the amount of the deposit shouldn't be a negotiating point in fulfilling the contingencies. It just confirms that you intend to get things moving, and that your offer is serious.

Standard earnest money and receipt forms used by real estate agents probably won't be adequate for a contingency deal. You'd have to delete many clauses and add others to suit your circumstances. It's better to have your lawyer start from scratch, or at least review an earnest money form prepared by the seller's attorney.

Try to arrange to negotiate a contingency contract *without* cash up front. To approach a potential seller with these terms, you need to satisfy them that you're bringing some expertise into the deal. Your experience in working with permit agencies is valuable. You can argue that your knowledge is worth more than a cash deposit. The owner wants to sell the land and you know how to get the plat approval (or you have someone on your payroll who does). Together, you both get what you want.

Instead of putting cash or a note into escrow, you agree to work with the seller to get through the regulatory maze downtown. You'll have to convince the owner that you're serious about buying the land and that you plan to start the ball rolling for plat approval as long as the owner agrees to sell the land to you later.

If the owner insists on an earnest money deposit, try to satisfy them with a promissory note instead of cash. Promissory notes are a common and effective way to bind a deal. Most initial deposits are covered by a signed note rather than handing over a check. Explain that money in an escrow account doesn't help you *or* the owner. The money isn't available — it just sits there, sometimes for years. A promissory note is just as effective as cash to bind your commitment to buy the land.

The Contract

Contracts can't be open-ended. Set specific deadlines to eliminate contingencies and determine feasibility. If it turns out that delays make a date unrealistic, you can amend the contract further by asking for more time. The seller will probably agree to an extension if circumstances beyond your control make this necessary.

Always consult your attorney about land deals and contracts, especially those which are contingent upon certain outcomes. Remember that every part of your agreement with a seller *must* be in writing. Verbal real estate agreements are never binding, so you need to protect yourself with legal and binding documents in case your contingencies don't pan out.

Use Options

An option is an agreement specifying some future performance (such as buying a property) in exchange for a benefit (such as cash). In other words, you give a seller money in exchange for the right to buy his land in the future.

Options are interesting because they let you control large amounts of land for relatively little cash up front. You might be able to secure an option with no cash at all! That's why developers like options.

As we've said, an earnest money agreement ties both sides to a deal that depends on performance by either or both parties, or meeting certain contingencies. By contrast, an option is an actual transaction and contract. You exchange money (or something else of value) for a right to buy land in the future at a specified price. The good thing about options is that you can design them in any way that's acceptable to you and the seller.

Options must always be in writing. And because they designate transfer of title, they've got to be recorded with your county as an attachment on the land, like a lien. That can't happen without full disclosure of all other holds and liens on the property.

A basic option works like this: You spot a piece of land that you expect will be ripe for development in the future — but you don't want to buy the land purely on speculation. Land is expensive, and you want to know before you actually buy it whether you can get zoning changes, financing, and so on. Options are a good tool in this case because by the time the land is ready for development, the price would probably be much higher than it is now. And someone else might buy it first.

You offer the owner a price for the *option* to buy the land. That price (the premium) buys you the right to buy the land at an agreed price and by a certain date. You can exercise the option by closing the sale at any time before the option deadline.

The price of an option depends on the market, the owner's eagerness to sell the property and how badly you want it. It's also affected by the price of the land and the length of time until the option expires.

As the deadline approaches, several things might happen to the value of the option:

▌ The conditions that you expected would make the property more valuable to you don't occur. You let the option expire in worthless condition — the seller keeps the land (and your option premium) and your option ceases to exist.

▌ The land value increases significantly and you exercise the option, but you pay the lower price determined in the option.

▌ The owner gets an offer to sell the property for more money than your option specifies, so he offers to buy back the option for more than you paid for it.

> **Example:** You buy an option on 85 acres, paying $8,500 for the right to buy the land for $1.2 million at any time in the next three years. At the end of the first year the landowner offers to buy back your option for $17,000.

It's pretty obvious that the owner has an offer over $1.2 million and wants to take it. But he can't accept that offer as long as you hold the option. The offered price is high enough that the seller is willing to let you double your money. You have three choices: refuse the offer, accept it, or make a counteroffer.

Get an option with no cash changing hands.

Here are some ways to get an option without paying up front:

▌ *Future profits:* You might agree to pay the current owner a percentage of future profits on the development.

▌ *Performance option:* In exchange for the right to buy the land by a specified date and for a specified price, you agree to work with governmental agencies to get the necessary plats, permits, reviews, and approvals. Sellers may agree to this if they realize that the only way to market the land is to complete these steps — and they're expensive steps the owner often would rather not take himself.

This choice doesn't require the rigid format and detailed contingency statements of the real estate contract because the option may not be exercised. But it does require action from both sides. You have to pay to get the approvals. And the seller agrees to sell you the land if you exercise the option.

▌ *Right of first refusal:* Similar to an ordinary option, this can buy you both time and money. You only have to exercise the option if and when someone else makes an offer on the property.

▌ *Letter of credit:* Another way to get an option without paying cash is through a letter of credit. Your bank agrees to provide contingent financing based on the land's value, and issues you a letter of credit. If you exercise the option, the seller agrees to settle up at the agreed price.

▌ *Property tax exchange:* You might also "finance" an option by agreeing to pay the owner's property taxes in exchange for the right to buy at a specified price by a specified date. This way, you keep the option alive as long as you make the property tax payments.

This even works if the taxes are due immediately and you don't want to tie up your money right away. Assessors usually won't foreclose on property until tax bills are at least a year or even two years old. You can let the deadline slip and pay the penalties and interest later, just before the foreclosure date.

The Rolling Option

The *rolling option* lets you spread an option over time. This is useful when a large parcel of land is available for development, but you can't afford to buy it all at once. The contract specifies that *all* the land is included in the option but you pay for the option in intervals. In the first phase, you pay for only part of the total and retain the right to pay premiums for additional parcels later.

This is more complex than a simple option, but it locks you in over many years. This gives the seller income over the time it takes to build your project, as long as you continue to pick up the options and exercise them. This may be attractive to the seller for income planning as well as tax purposes.

> **Example:** A current owner is willing to sell 600 residentially-zoned acres. You can't afford to buy that much land now, but you know there will be a market for your housing development over the next 10 years or more. You identify 10 parcels of 60 acres each.

If you don't exercise your rights under the option, the whole commitment is canceled and the seller keeps the premium.

You offer a rolling option with certain conditions. First, all 600 acres are included at a specified price, as long as you meet all the specified payment deadlines. If you miss a deadline, the seller can cancel the deal.

An initial deposit gives you the right to acquire the first 60 acres within one year for a specified price. You agree to pay an additional premium at the end of the first year that ties up the second 60 acres for one year from the payment date. You further agree to continue rolling from one year to the next over the next 10 years.

As the buyer, you have a guarantee of an orderly development opportunity. It makes sense to develop 60 acres per year and let the market absorb the units as they're built, while 600 acres of new housing might be too much to expect to sell — let alone build — all at once.

The 1031 Exchange

If you already own investment property, you can exchange it without immediate tax consequences for other land that's more appropriate for your development. This is called a "1031 exchange," a reference to Internal Revenue Code section 1031 which spells out the rules for tax-free exchanges.

The term "tax-free exchange" isn't quite accurate. (I don't think there's any such thing as really tax-free.) The tax-free aspect of this exchange doesn't mean that the taxes disappear; they're just postponed. When you sell the developed land, you have to pay taxes on two gains, one from sale of the previous property (the deferred gain), the other on the profit from the sale of the developed property.

> **Example:** Let's say you own some property — raw land, a house, apartment building, commercial property — and you want to sell it to finance another project. When you bought the property many years ago, it cost next to nothing. But if you sell it, you'll have to pay a huge capital gains tax. So you've avoided an outright sale.

Many development projects never happen because the tax consequences of selling existing land would eat up all the profits.

This is where a tax-free exchange saves the day. You can sell one property and buy another "like-kind" property without paying taxes on the increased value of the land you sold. Like-kind means the properties you sell and buy are generally the same kind. Investment and development real estate is all like-kind under the law. That means you can exchange between residential, commercial, industrial, raw land, etc., and it all counts under the definition of "like-kind" property. Of course, there's an exception: You can't transact property through a 1031 exchange if there's an option written on the property.

You can sell the property you own now and buy another, but you have to make the purchase within six months of the sale. The property you buy has to cost at least as much as you get for the property you sell.

Your real estate contract must specify that the owner of the land you're buying is cooperating with you in a 1031 exchange. And you're required by federal law to channel the transactions through a facilitator who's a third party not involved in the transaction.

This person files the paperwork for both sides, makes sure that deadlines are met, and that the subject properties meet the federal qualifications. Some attorneys or accountants set up businesses just to act as facilitators. You can find them through banks, real estate offices or by asking other accountants and lawyers.

As you can see, you have to jump through several hoops to make the tax-free exchange work. Some of the hoops don't make a lot of sense to anyone but tax agents, and the rules include precise restrictions on what you can do during the six months between the time you sell your property and buy a new one. For instance, you can't receive any money for the property you're exchanging until the exchange is concluded. Proceeds from the sale of your property remain in escrow with the facilitator until they're passed to the owner of the property you're buying. The six-month time limit keeps these exchanges from pending indefinitely.

The mechanics and details of executing a deal like this are too complex to cover here. Even if you've experienced this type of transaction, always get advice from an expert for any 1031 exchange.

You need more than just a good accountant when you're involved in creative financing methods. You'll probably need expert advice from a mortgage banker or real estate lawyer, as well as the facilitator. A guardian angel might help, too. It's not exactly a do-it-yourself procedure.

It's never easy to get money. It's even harder to launch a project without borrowing money or laying out large amounts of cash up front. But that's the way developers often get through the initial planning, site location and commitment phases of their projects. Creative financing alternatives aren't easy. But it's usually worth the effort to come up with a financing option that works for both you and the seller, and lets you put off spending your cash as long as you can.

Chapter 6

Write Your Business Plan

Even if you've succeeded in getting a commitment for your land without cash up front, you'll probably need financing at some point in your development project. And the first thing an investor or lender will want to see is your project business plan.

Every project needs a plan. Without a plan, not only won't you know where you're going, you won't even know if you're lost! There's a lot of wisdom in the maxim, "No one plans to fail, they only fail to plan." In this chapter you'll learn the steps that go into preparing your business plan. Appendix A, in the back of the book, is a sample business plan that you can use as a model.

Your business plan isn't just a lot of numbers that tell about what you do. It reflects *you* — it gives the lender an insight into who you are and what you value. Business people don't like to admit to relying on intuition, but the fact is that we make many decisions based on our hunches. Lenders are no exception. Make sure the plan has your "voice" and reveals the best features of your character and personality.

Write your plan yourself.

Write your plan yourself for the same reasons you did your own market study. You learn a lot from gathering, organizing and presenting the information that describes your project and your business. The plan isn't complicated. Your accountant may furnish some of the documents you'll need to make your case, but write the interpretation yourself. Once you've done that, you can have your accountant review it.

Under the law, lenders can't discriminate against borrowers based on race, religion, sex, or age. But loan decisions ultimately rest on discriminating — between good risks and bad risks, between successful track records and less-than-successful ones, and between borrowers whose business plans are compelling and others whose plans are vague or incomplete.

Definition

A business plan is a forecast, a budget, and a projection.

An ordinary business plan most often describes a company's budget and marketing plan for the coming year. Our plan describes an entire project which depends on getting financing to make it work. The plan is a forecast (of income and costs), a budget (of expenses) and a projection (of future cash flow). It's a blueprint of how you expect your financial future to look.

A good plan is:

▌ Based on information gathered from past experience.

▌ Your best prediction of what will happen in the future.

▌ Flexible, and subject to correction as new information becomes available.

Your business plan is the final, summarized version of all the research information you've compiled. The business plan reveals business information the same way financial statements do. You couldn't easily judge how well a company is doing by looking inside their filing cabinet filled with a full year's bookkeeping transactions. You'd need a summary that focuses on the bottom line.

That's what your business plan does. It helps the lender judge the shape of your business and your vision of the future.

The business plan lets you demonstrate how clearly you view the future.

Your job is to supervise the creation and execution of the plan. You need *super vision* about the future — not how it *might* come out based on just numbers, but how you can turn your vision into reality through planning.

Purpose

Your plan is the document that will convince your lender that it's a smart business decision to grant you a loan.

A short plan is better than a long one. The rules are the same as for a professional résumé. First impressions count. Your lender will lose interest if they have to hunt through pages of narrative to get the facts about what you're doing. And a lender or investor who has a stack of competing business plans on their desk will often pick through the stack and read the short ones first!

Your business plan's main purpose is to:

▌ Describe your business and your project, simply and honestly.

▌ Demonstrate that you've come up with a profitable idea.

▌ Prove that you know how to control and manage your business.

▌ Cover all the questions you expect the lender to ask.

▌ Confront your risks and show that you know how to overcome them.

Besides presenting your case to the lender, the business plan's second (and possibly more important) function is to give you a way to keep your expanded business on the right path. You can write the best plan in the world, but once you begin to follow it, you'll run into bumps and potholes that throw you off the track. So review your plan regularly. Compare it to actual performance so you can react quickly and make necessary corrections before small problems become big ones. We'll discuss that further in Chapter 10.

Preparation

As you prepare to assemble your plan, first gather and organize all the data you've collected so far. Sit down with your market studies and sum up the facts that apply to your project. Be sure you're ready to answer every question the lender might ask you.

Your Market

Extract from your market study all the information that relates specifically to your project. You must be able to describe your potential market with great clarity. If you plan to build houses, you need to describe the housing market as it applies to the size and price of housing you plan to build.

▮ How many homes like this are already on the market?

▮ How long do they stay on the market?

▮ Who is buying them?

▮ What are buyers paying for them?

▮ Which age segment of the population are you targeting?

▮ How many of those people are there?

▮ How many of those people earn enough to buy your houses?

If you plan to build commercial or industrial buildings, your market will naturally be quite different. But the answers you want from your market study will be similar.

▮ How many units are already available?

▮ Do occupants buy or lease?

▮ Who is the customer base (commercial) or employee pool (industrial).

If you plan to keep the developed property and lease it, you need to demonstrate not only a demand for the property, but also that the lease income will cover your expenses as well as pay off the loan. The lender will want to know how you identified the vacancy factor, especially in multiple-unit developments. Better yet, find out what factor the lender uses, and build that into your plan.

Your Project Site

What's so great about this site?

Here's where you pull together the facts you need to "sell" your site selection to the lender. Summarize the information from your land market study and the details you added from the additional questions you answered in Chapter 4.

▌ Why did you choose this particular parcel over the others you considered?

Of course, price is important. And it's easy to do the math that proves that one lot is a better buy than another. But location can be just as important. You'll need to convince the lender that the site you've chosen is appropriate and convenient for your development plan. Zoning, access, surrounding uses and the path of progress may all influence your choice of the most suitable location for your project.

▌ Describe the site's physical features.

Here are some examples: If it's for housing, does it offer views? Does the topography permit separation and privacy for individual or groups of dwellings? Open space for a golf course or park? For an industrial project, describe rail or highway proximity. For a commercial development, call attention to site attributes which contribute to access or parking.

▌ Does the development affect adjacent property owners?

Whenever more than one owner is involved in development or affected by its course, a master plan may be required. How much will that cost? How long will it take to get the master plan drawn and approved? Will the other owners cooperate with you and share the expense? A lender will be very interested to know whether you have friendly and cooperative neighbors, or if there's organized opposition.

▌ How much have you budgeted for mitigation of environmental impact?

Depending on the nature of your project and the habitat within the boundaries of your land — not to mention waterways or protected areas — mitigation could be a major expense. You might also have to provide noise or open space buffers between your project and others nearby, especially if your site borders on a residential area. Buffer zones protect neighboring areas from noise and ugly views.

They also protect waterways within the site from potential environmental damage. You may need to assign a significant portion of your overall land space to buffer zones. Quote guidelines from your local environmental protection office describing likely requirements for your project.

▌ List in detail what you have to do to make the land ready for development, and what that will cost.

Describe such things as grading, paving, providing services, and other preparatory operations. If the ground isn't level, how much grading is required? Grading is expensive, so be sure you know up front how much it will cost.

▌ If no existing roads or utilities exist, how do you plan to pay for those basic services?

Can you organize other owners in the area to participate in (and help pay for) water, sewers, and roads? Or will you carry the costs by yourself? How long will it take to provide services? What approvals will you need?

Goals and Assumptions

Your development plan started out as an idea. But it takes action to turn ideas into reality:

▌ You've probably already set some specific goals and a proposed date for their completion.

▌ You based these goals on certain assumptions.

Your research into available land and the probable demand for your proposed project, along with your experience and financial situation, have provided the facts to back up (or revise) those assumptions. In order for your goals to be practical, your assumptions have to be based on facts.

Put your goals and assumptions in writing.

If you haven't already done so, now is the time to *write down* your goals and assumptions. This will help confirm your ideas in your own mind, and prepare you to discuss them clearly with your prospective lender when you present your business plan.

Remember that goals aren't just dreams or wishes. They must be realistic intentions that you can accomplish in a series of measurable steps. Focus each goal on a single end result and make it specific. Set a target date for every goal. Relate each goal to the assumption(s) that make it practical.

Dave may have taken too literally the book's advice that you make
the goals in your business plan concise and honest.

Examples of goals are:

▌ Locate within one month a site suitable for development of 40 single-family homes.

▌ Complete within three months a detailed business plan for a 40-unit tract.

▌ Hire five new journeyman electricians by the end of next month.

In the last example, the assumption would be that there are plenty of journeyman electricians available. You might get supporting data from the local electrician's union, employment office or newspaper classified section.

Word your assumptions as briefly and plainly as possible. Then list the facts and figures from your land and market studies that back them up. Be sure to reference your sources for the facts you quote. We all know how to make up or embellish facts to support our cause, and a lender knows this. So either attach the referenced report or article to your business plan, or have a copy available if the lender requests it.

> **Example:** Employment of blue-collar workers in this area will rise by 2,000 within the next two years, creating greater demand for new housing.

If you put that statement into your business plan without any supporting data, your lender might dispute it as opinion alone. So back all your statements up with facts about predicted local company expansions or news that a major employer is moving to your area. Use information from your land or market study to justify every assumption.

Here are some other examples of assumptions:

▌ There's a growing market in this community for additional single-family housing in a price range between $150,000 and $225,000.

▌ There are numerous competitively-priced land sites for sale in the area.

▌ My company's expertise and financial standing are sound enough to assure loan approval for land purchase and development.

Use a form like the one in Figure 6-1 to summarize your goals and assumptions.

Equipment

List any new equipment you'll have to acquire or upgrade in order to complete the project. This could include anything from computers to Caterpillars. Indicate whether additional equipment costs will depend on the loan proceeds. Make a shopping list for make, model, price, source, and so on.

Facilities

Describe your present physical business space, and changes you expect will be necessary to accommodate the development project. Include your job site temporary office and storage buildings, dumpsters, toilet facilities, etc. Then indicate whether you'll pay for these with current capital, or if you'll require loan proceeds to increase facilities.

Personnel

List any investors or partners you have in this project, and to what extent they're involved. (We'll talk about how to recruit them in Chapter 7.)

Summarize the job descriptions, pay scales, and number of workers on your payroll. Show which job slots you'll fill by hiring during the project, both trade workers and office personnel.

List the subcontractors you'll use to supplement your own crews during the project. Specify which trade specialists you'll need, and for how long.

You can use current employment statistics covering available workers in the job market, along with their average pay rates to judge whether employee turnover may present problems for you during the project.

Goal number:		Completion date:	
Description:			
Assumptions:		Location of supporting data:	
1.			
2.			
3.			
4.			
Steps to complete goal:		Due	Complete
1.			
2.			
3.			
4.			
5.			

Figure 6-1 Goals and assumptions worksheet

Suppliers

Make a list of your current suppliers and subs. Survey them ahead of time to see if they can handle your expanded requirements.

Line up new sources to supplement the ones you've been using so you won't be caught in a bind if one of them fails to perform.

Draw Your Plans

By now your engineers and drafters should be busy preparing the working blueprints for the project. Make a set of floor plans and elevations to illustrate the homes, stores, offices or factories that will make up the development. Use it when you present your plan to the lender or investor.

Begin Your Takeoffs

You'll need takeoffs before you can begin pricing materials, services and equipment for the project. You need this information before you can complete the Forecast and Budget and the *Pro forma* Income Statement.

Schedule the Project

Set up your project schedule. This has to be fairly detailed so you can accurately determine your cash requirements as the project moves forward. Your schedule forms the basis for the Forecast and Budget and the Cash Flow Projection — it determines when and how much funding you'll need.

Resolve Zoning and Permit Issues

Do a thorough job when you prepare to present your case for a rezone, conditional-use permit, or variance. Your lender will want to know that you've succeeded in settling all the legal issues.

Have the necessary maps on hand. Anticipate the questions you'll face from the zoning and planning agencies and be prepared to answer them with facts, not emotional arguments. You need to convince politicians and planners that your idea is a "good" idea on two levels: First, it will benefit the community. Second, it'll make the politicians look good, too.

Use arguments that address local issues. Here are a few examples:

- This development won't affect any agricultural land.
- My (industrial or commercial) project will bring (specify number) jobs to this community.
- Traffic from my housing tract won't strain the capacity of existing arterial roads or highways.
- Sales tax revenue from my commercial project will add (specify amount) dollars to the city's income.

Get Bids from Suppliers and Subcontractors

Start getting bids to confirm and fine-tune your materials and labor estimates. Get a commitment from each bidder as to how long the prices remain in effect. Keep all the bids on hand, even those from vendors who aren't your "first line" suppliers. You can use these as backups in case your primary sources don't come through as expected.

It's possible that your lender may want to see a list of your vendors, and could even require that loan proceeds be paid directly to suppliers or subs.

Confirm Your Selling Price

Never set the price for your development just to make your plan's assumptions work out. Study current selling prices for developments like yours and see if you can compete based on your cost estimates. That way, you'll see at once if your plan is realistic.

If your plan *isn't* realistic, it's time to make a different plan! That doesn't mean you'll cut corners on materials or quality. It means you might have to reassess the market, your competition, and your own competitive and financial strength. Only when you're sure your project will sell, based on reliable information, should you attempt to move on — especially with borrowed money.

Review your market study to find out how long properties like yours remain on the market. Review the spread between listed and actual selling prices. Those are both good indicators of how strong the demand is for your project. These demand factors (and a little clairvoyance) will indicate whether you'll get your asking price when your project is finished.

Content

You've got piles of information. Now it's time to condense and organize it into the package you'll take to the bank or your potential investors.

By the time you're through preparing the plan, you'll be able to recite it in your sleep.

You build your business plan the same way you build a house: from the ground up. But the order in which you present it is just the reverse. You start by showing the finished product (the number of rooms and their arrangement) and cover the details later (the foundation, walls, roof, fixtures and cosmetics).

Someone who buys your house won't necessarily demand to see the details of how the plumbing was installed. They just want to know it's *there* and that it passed inspection. It's the same with the lender. They want to see the big picture first, then consider the details later.

The business plan is a flexible document that's subject to many revisions. If you don't use a computer, hire someone who does to keyboard your business plan for you. It's much easier to update a computer file and print a page or two than to retype pages of text or numbers.

Use the computer for project scheduling also. Project management software offers a flexible and convenient way to control a complex schedule and to automatically adjust for slips in "critical path" events — those which must be finished before the next operation can begin.

Reference your sources as efficiently as you can without cluttering up your report. Use footnotes if you have to, but it's better if you cite brief references in the business plan as captions to the facts the references support.

Place your opinions or comments with the facts that justify them. Most people find that less distracting than to look for a footnote at the bottom of the page, then try to find their place again.

By the time you're through preparing the plan, you'll be able to recite it in your sleep. But your lender hasn't seen it before and may not be familiar with you or your business. Make it easy to spot significant information at a glance.

Packaging

A three-ring binder is efficient because it lets you develop and change your plan as things move along. A business plan, like a properly-used budget, is never really finished. It changes constantly, so you want to be able to revise it easily. A nice touch is to use a binder with a clear vinyl pocket on the front for the cover page.

- Use a type style that's easy to read. Set headings in bold type, larger than the main text.

- Pay attention to grammar, punctuation and spelling so the reader won't doubt your professionalism and dismiss your application for possibly-irrelevant reasons.

- Use labeled, tabbed divider sheets between the major sections.

- Stick with white paper, at least 20-pound weight. Anything lighter than that lets the print from the following page show through. And avoid glossy paper — it creates a glare.

- Print on only one side of the paper. That's less distracting for the reader. Surround headings and paragraphs with white space. Use wide margins (at least 1¼ inch at the bound side, 1 inch outside).

- Make enough copies for your lender's loan committee (call ahead to find out how many), plus one or two more in case other bank officers decide to sit in on their meeting. Keep a copy for yourself, of course, and have two or three more in reserve.

- Cross reference and label everything. Make it easy for the reader to find the assumptions, illustrations, evidence and supporting information that backs up every statement you make. This thorough approach will demonstrate that you're a well-organized, skilled manager.

Cover Page

The cover page should have only the following information on it:

- The words "Business Plan"

- Your company name (and logo if you have one)

- Date the plan was prepared

- Copy number

- Disclaimer (if appropriate) or confidentiality statement

The cover letter which accompanies your loan package is where you identify yourself personally and show your company address, telephone number, fax number, e-mail address, Web site, and any other information.

On the date line, show only the year, or the month and year, so the plan won't appear outdated if you give it to someone several weeks or months after you prepare it.

Keep a log of the copies you distribute. Make up a code for the copy number instead of just numbering them sequentially. You may pass out copies to several lenders, brokers, or potential investors. It looks better if they get Copy L-2 or Copy P-1, not Copy 22, which may look like you're papering the town with your plan.

You can include a "prepared for" entry on the cover page showing the lender's name to personalize your presentation. Then if that lender turns you down, you only have to change that page before you send the package to someone else.

Table of Contents

List each heading and attachment. Number the pages so your reader can find things easily.

Summary: What Am I Doing?

This is a brief explanation of the plan's purpose. Keep it short. Let the lender know how much you need, what you'll use the money for, and how and when you'll pay it back. Reference the section and page number where the reader will find the supporting details.

Make this as brief as you can, but make it easy for the reader to find what they want.

Briefly list each of your assumptions that make this project practical. Reference your market and land studies or other facts you collected during the preparation steps.

Show the project's duration. List the top-level events from your project calendar or schedule, then attach the project plan to the business plan.

You have two choices of format for your summary information:

1. A synopsis lists just the facts about your operating detail without much commentary. It may be a bit dry, but it has the advantage of being brief.

2. A narrative with more emphasis on your operating philosophy and your company's distinctive features. It gives more depth and insight than a synopsis, but takes a little longer for the reader to digest.

The difference between the two might be compared to what you use when you plan a vacation: The synopsis is like an itinerary; the narrative is your travel guide.

Here's how to prepare a synopsis:

- Describe your company, its name, specialty, and legal status.

- State your long-term goals — where you see your company going.

- Describe your company's background and stage of development.

- Define your project, target market and marketing strategy.

- Specify how much money you need.

- Analyze your competition and the advantages you can claim over them.

- List the members of your management team and describe their capabilities.

- Describe your "exit strategy." What happens once the project is finished?

You might plan to pay off the lender or partner, then take your profit. Or you might intend to roll the profits into a new development, either alone or with your partner(s). Or maybe you intend to sell your company outright and move on to something different.

The business plan you create for your own use should cover your exit plan in detail. The one you present to a lender or investor only needs to show how you intend to repay a loan or compensate partners.

A narrative summary gives the same information, but the outline for preparing it is a little different. Remember that you're writing an essay in this case, whereas the synopsis is more like an outline. Be sure to include:

- A detailed description of your company, including its stage of development

- The concepts that drive your company — set it apart from others like it and make it unique

- Market opportunities that point to the success of your development project

- Your competitive advantage

- Your management team's virtues

- Milestones or achievements in your company's history

- Financial summary: How much cash you need, whether you have other investors and how much they're in for, how you'll use the money, and how you'll pay it back.

The summary in Appendix A (Sample Business Plan) is an example of the narrative form. Figure 6-2 shows the same information in a synopsis format.

How Much Do I Need?

The next page in your business plan is the *pro forma* income statement. Your annual income statement presents information about past operations in the format:

	Income
less	Costs
Equals	Gross Profit
less	Expenses
Equals	Net Profit

The *pro forma* statement illustrates what the *future* will look like based on a series of assumptions. Explain every line in the *pro forma* statement with references to your goals, assumptions, cash flow projection, forecast and budget.

Unlike typical financial statements, the *pro forma* may be for a period other than a year. It should cover the expected duration of your project.

The assumptions reflected in the *pro forma* statement include:

▌ Getting the loan

▌ Using the money to buy the land and pay for development costs

▌ Finishing the project on time

▌ Staying within the budget

▌ Selling or leasing the project at a profit

No *pro forma* estimate will be accurate down to the nearest penny. That isn't its purpose. The reason for "crunching the numbers" is to demonstrate how you plan to use borrowed money to increase profits, and provide the lender with information to judge you, your business, and your development plan.

How Will I Use the Money?

This is where you prove (or disprove) that your project will succeed and make money. You need to anticipate in detail how the money will flow into and out of your business during the time before the development begins to produce income. Include only the following two reports in your business plan. Reference the detail worksheets containing the assumptions that led to the statements. Either append the worksheets to your business plan as attachments, or note that they're available by request.

Describe your company, its name, specialty, and legal status

Anderson Development, Inc., incorporated in 1996, specializes in single-family residential construction.

State your long-term goals — where you see your company going

Our goal for the future is to become a significant competitor in the development market, competing with other developers with gross incomes ranging from $1 to $20 million.

Describe your company's background and stage of development

The owners of Anderson Development have been active in the local business community for more than 20 years. The current project is an extension of our history of single-family custom building and remodeling.

Define your project, target market and marketing strategy

The current project, for which we seek financing, involves development of 40 acres into 90 single-family homes to be completed over the following 12 months, and selling in the range of $185,000 to $210,000. We have contracted with County Homes, Inc. for exclusive rights to sell the project.

Specify how much money you need and how you'll pay it back

We are applying for a loan of $2 million, with repayment to begin in month 4 after start of construction. We expect to retire the entire loan within 12 months of breaking ground. Funds will be used for land acquisition, development of services and construction.

Analyze your competition and the advantages you can claim over them

Because we are a small company compared to our competitors, the owners can provide a hands-on approach and stay in touch with all aspects of our operation. In larger companies, there is a tendency for top management to lose touch with day-to-day operations. Although we are smaller, we have demonstrated our ability to manage cash flow and capital assets well.

List the members of your management team and describe their capabilities

President and CEO — over 25 years of experience in the trades and several years as owner of his own company; a thorough knowledge of planning, scheduling, estimating and construction; and a degree in engineering.

Vice President, Chief Estimator — more than 20 years of field experience, including on-site management, budgeting, and planning connected to development; worked for several years for a residential real estate corporation.

Vice President, Operations — more than 20 years as superintendent of field operations for a major construction firm; has been with the organization since inception.

Describe your "exit strategy." What happens once the project is finished?

Upon completion of the units, our initial goal must be to sell the properties, and to avoid accumulating an undesirable equity position in so many units that our cash flow begins to suffer. Upon successful completion and sale of all the units, we plan to investigate further projects.

Figure 6-2 Business plan introduction

Forecast and Budget

The forecast is your future sales and direct costs and the budget is your estimate of future overhead expense. Together they're a monthly breakdown of your *pro forma* income statement. Show figures by the month with quarterly subtotals because that's how you'll review actual expenses later when you compare them to your forecasts. Identify the months as 1 through 12, because if delays occur in getting financing or starting construction, the time line will continue to apply. Prepare the forecast and budget to cover the time you expect the project to take, but not less than a year. Review the budget at least every six months, and update it if necessary.

Remember that the farther ahead you try to estimate the financial outcome, the less reliable your forecast will be. To prove that, just think about your own financial expectations over the past couple of years. Too many variables enter the picture and muddy things up. That's why a two- to five-year forecast and budget is a complete waste of time.

Make long-range plans in written-out goals, but don't bother to try to crunch the numbers beyond one to two years at the very most.

So how can you forecast a development that will take longer than that? The answer is, you can't. And the lender knows that. The solution is to break down forecasts into shorter-term units.

> **Example:** A 500-unit subdivision that will be done in four phases may take five years. A 125-house increment may be done in about 15 months and it's easy to forecast that. Based on the similarity between increments, you can reasonably forecast longer-term costs, expenses and profits based on the more easily-estimated initial phase.

You can apply the same principle to more complex projects, budgets and forecasts. Break the job into phases or increments. Then show how those individual "chunks" can be managed profitably if you follow the forecast guidelines.

Budgets are based on certain assumptions. Be sure those assumptions make sense. For example, base your budget for telephone expense on usage:

▮ The number of phone lines to your office and job site(s)

▮ Whether you provide callers with a toll-free number

▮ Current billing rates for local, toll and long distance calls

▮ Choice of billing options — unlimited local calling at a higher base rate vs. a lower base rate but a charge for every call

▮ Number of cell phones or pagers and how they're used

Base each expense on assumptions you can track later, so if actual expenses vary from the budget, you can easily spot the cause.

Start each year's budget fresh — never base it on the past year. Don't just use last year's expense and raise it by a percentage. That isn't a budget. All that does is build last year's mistakes into this year's forecast.

Study last year's budget only to see how close you came to actual expenses and identify overruns. Start from zero in each expense category. Then break each category into its components. Research each component to see if you can streamline procedures to cut costs, or if new demands will *increase* expenses during the budget term.

Cash Flow Projection

Profit and loss is never the whole story. Too often the "profit" in your business — income less costs and expenses — doesn't explain what's really going on when there's no cash available to pay the current month's bills.

There are a couple of ways to measure cash flow:

▌ Current ratio = current assets ÷ current liabilities

▌ Working capital = cash equivalents – current liabilities

Current assets are cash or assets that will be converted to cash within one year (such as accounts receivable and inventory).

Current liabilities are liabilities payable within one year (like accounts payable, taxes owed, and 12 months' payments due on loans).

The *current ratio* is is a good measure of cash health. A ratio of 2 to 1 or better is considered minimally acceptable in businesses that carry inventory. If you don't carry inventory, a 1 to 1 ratio is generally acceptable. A ratio less than that (where liabilities are more than assets) indicates problems with the business.

> **Example:** With assets of $528,762 and current liabilities of $211,515, the current ratio is 2.5 to 1:
>
> 528,762 ÷ 211,515 = 2.4998

You can run out of cash to fund operations even when profits are high. Here are some causes:

▌ Greater outstanding accounts receivable

▌ Increased inventory

▌ Decrease in liabilities (accounts payable)

▌ Early payoff of existing loans

▌ Purchase of capital assets (real estate other than land, equipment and machinery, furniture and fixtures, etc.)

Each of these means less money in your checkbook even though your profit doesn't change.

Cash flow projections show the lender that you've planned how you'll pay for land, materials and equipment acquisition costs, and loan principal and interest out of current funds; and that you're aware of expected changes in assets and liabilities.

The cash flow projection looks just like your cash flow statement, showing sources of funds and when and how you'll spend them. Carry forward the net change for each month to the beginning of the following month.

How Will I Pay It Back?

Who Are My Clients (Sale or Lease?)

Copy the information you condensed during the preparation phase described earlier in this chapter under *Your Market*.

Selling the Project

How will you attract potential buyers to your project? Here are some examples of questions you need to answer:

- Where will you advertise? On radio? TV? On the Internet? In neighboring communities? Billboards on the site? Newspapers?
- How much will you budget for advertising?
- Will someone from your office handle sales, or will you contract with a Realtor™ or broker?
- How much will you pay in commissions?
- To what extent will you furnish and landscape models?
- Will you hold any units to lease or rent?
- Will you carry any of the buyers' mortgages yourself?

Answer all these questions well in advance. All the answers have financial implications that you want to be aware of ahead of time. There's nothing worse than having to say later on, "I didn't think it was going to cost us that much to sell this project."

Financial Statements — Evidence of Past Performance

The business plan is a forward-looking document. But financial statements reveal how successful you've been in reaching your goals in the past. For example, if your overall standard is to retain a 5 percent net profit every year, you can measure that — it shows up on your income statement.

You might change that standard in the future, but while it's in effect you can measure performance against it. You'll learn:

- Whether or not your goal is realistic

■ Whether or not you reached your goal, and if not, why not

■ How and why to change your course in the future

Bankers think they can tell a lot about your business management skills by reviewing your recent financial statements. Your accountant prepares three financial statements each fiscal year. They cover a one-year period. Include at least the most recent set in your business plan. The lender will probably want to see the statements for the previous two years also.

The financial statements are records of your recent business history. They're most valuable when presented in comparative format. That means that you show this year's results of operations in the first column and the previous year's results in the second column. This way the lender can see how one year's operations went compared to another.

If your comparative statement shows a decline in your business condition last year compared to the year before, you'll need to reveal that and explain to the lender what caused it to happen.

Here are the financial statements you'll include in your business plan:

■ Balance Sheet: Shows as of a specific date (usually the end of a quarter or year) the values of your assets, liabilities and net worth. Assets are things you own, such as properties, cash, accounts receivable, inventory, equipment, deposits, etc. Liabilities are what you owe. Net worth is the difference between the two.

■ Income Statement: Reports income, costs and expenses over the period ending with the preparation of the balance sheet.

■ Statement of Cash Flows: Reveals how long-term assets and liabilities have changed over time (usually the same period as that reported on the income statement). This shows how working capital (the net difference between current assets and current liabilities) was used during the period to increase or decrease the balances in other accounts. For example, using cash to buy capital equipment (machinery, automobiles and trucks, furniture and fixtures, etc.), paying down long-term notes, buying real estate, or drawing out profits.

Your accountant or CPA will furnish a letter or document similar to Figure 6-3, certifying that they have prepared the documents based on information from your company's bookkeeping system. Insert a copy of this letter at the beginning of the Financial Statements section of your business plan.

To Whom It May Concern:

I prepared the enclosed balance sheet, income statement and statement of cash flows from the books and records of [your company name]. I have performed annual full audits on the company and quarterly full reviews. In my opinion, the books and records reflect an accurate summary of the condition and transactions of the corporation, and conform to generally accepted auditing standards.

The latest results as reflected in these statements were taken directly from the books and records of the company, and are a compilation only. These are not meant to represent a complete or full audit of the books and records.

[Signed by the CPA]

Figure 6-3 CPA certification letter

What to Leave Out

Everything in your business plan should lead to a decision that will assure that your project goes forward. Omit anything that doesn't apply directly to the purpose of the plan, which is to convince the lender to advance the cash.

▌ Leave out anything provided by anyone not intimately familiar with your business, unless it helps support points *you* want to make. For instance, demographic statistics from your Chamber of Commerce might be appropriate, while survey results relating to commercial occupancy rates may not apply if your project is to build houses.

▌ Don't include anything that doesn't enlighten the reader about your business, your skills, and your immediate plans. Avoid criticizing your competitors, or bemoaning the unfriendly attitude of planning authorities. Such statements may label you as one who blames their problems on others rather than acting positively to solve them. That makes lenders nervous!

Presentation

A professionally-written business plan strikes a balance between excessive volume and full disclosure. The fewer pages there are in your plan, the better your chances that the lender will read all of it. But the less information you give, the less effective it is. So keep your plan as short as you can and use references and attachments to fill in the details.

This is like the technique accountants use when they prepare financial statements. The statement is a one-page overview. The ledger contains monthly summaries. Journals list transaction totals. And finally, the individual invoices, receipts and canceled checks are the source for all the entries in the system. Each step in the paper trail contains less information, but gives more clarity.

Supporting Attachments

If you cite reports at length, attach those reports (or excerpts) to your business plan. If the volume of information is too much to make this practical, note in your plan that the referenced materials are available on request. Be sure you have a copy of all the sources you cite in your report so you can duplicate more if you need them.

Make available any other documents that support the business plan. Examples include the detailed worksheets you used to develop your income and cost forecast, expense budget, or cash flow projections.

These worksheets may cover many pages, so don't include them in the plan itself. But the lender might want to track your conclusions back to the detail that leads to the summaries in your business plan.

Include copies of your business and personal tax returns and financial statements for at least the previous two years.

Your lender may want to see your entire market study. Ask whether you should include it, or if your summary information is enough.

If you attach material supplied by your land use consultant or attorney, be sure you thoroughly understand those documents so you can discuss them with confidence.

Show and Tell

You'll have to know your plan forward, backward and inside out before you present it to your lender or investor. Be ready for questions. Prepare yourself to answer those questions positively and without hesitation.

And don't forget to bring maps and drawings of your project showing its location, exterior elevations and floor plans. You know what a good picture is worth!

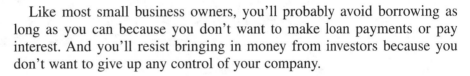

Chapter 7

Investors

Like most small business owners, you'll probably avoid borrowing as long as you can because you don't want to make loan payments or pay interest. And you'll resist bringing in money from investors because you don't want to give up any control of your company.

But we already know that expanding your business into land development is nearly impossible if you can't get someone else to help you finance it. Unless you have a generous rich uncle willing to back your expansion with no strings attached, you'll eventually have to deal with the troubling question of how to find the money you need to develop land.

By now you've found a site for your project. If the owner won't work with you and you don't own other real estate you can exchange for the new property, you still have some choices besides borrowing to raise cash. With your newly-completed and polished business plan and sales strategy in hand, consider these options:

▮ Find an active partner to give you cash in exchange for a share of your company's net worth (equity) and to help you run the business.

▮ Sell part of your equity to a silent partner who doesn't want to take part in day-to-day management but will still receive some of your future profits.

▮ Incorporate your business and sell shares.

▮ Enter into a joint venture which ends with the current project.

Different kinds of partners have different goals and expectations. Silent partners don't take part in day-to-day management. Their risk is limited to the amount of money they invest.

On the other hand, general partners are probably looking for a working relationship and will want to be involved in everyday operations. They'll want to be paid well, not only for their investment money, but also for their time and expertise. They become part owner and employee of the company, just like you. They also expose themselves to more risk because they could be responsible for debts or judgments far in excess of their investment.

Dave triumphed silently to himself, "And the book said that wealthy
investors who are foolish with their money are hard to find.
Ha! I found me one."

Be sure your "house is in order" before you begin to look for an investor. Never consider equity capital as an alternative to borrowing only because you've been slow paying your bills and your credit standing is weak. Your first priority should be to correct the problem by following these steps:

1. Take stock. See how much you owe and what it will take to pay it back.

2. Put yourself on a budget. Resolve to use a specific amount or percentage of profits every month to pay off past due bills.

3. Don't borrow any more or increase your accounts payable.

4. Consider a consolidation loan if that will help you get your monthly payments under control.

5. Stick to the plan. It might take months (or years) to solve your credit problems. But don't try to expand your business or go into land development until you have your finances well in hand. Land development isn't a way to get out of debt!

Only then should you even consider looking for new capital, either by borrowing or by selling equity. Be sure your business is running solidly in the black before you attempt to recruit investors.

Wealthy investors who are foolish with their money are hard to find. The first thing potential investors will do is check your credit record. They know that if you join forces, your credit rating can affect theirs. They may conclude from a bad credit history that you're not a good business manager and therefore a poor risk for investment. (And in a lot of cases, they'd be right!)

Equity Capital Pros and Cons

"Equity capital" means you sell part of your company's value (net worth) in exchange for cash. There are significant differences between bringing in investors and getting a loan.

It's true that both solve your immediate need for money. But the differences show up in the long-term consequences. Loans are eventually repaid. The payments might strain cash flow during the term of the loan, but your full ownership remains intact when the loan is paid off. When you get cash by selling equity, you don't have to repay a loan because there isn't one. But be aware of the tradeoffs.

Equity Capital Benefits

You don't pay interest to investors. When you borrow money, interest (and sometimes repayment) usually starts immediately. Even if you've arranged for deferred payment, you eventually pay interest from the time you got the cash.

Remember that interest erodes profits. Most analysts track a company's success by looking at profit as a percentage of sales. As sales increase and overhead levels out, your percentage of net profit should rise, or at least remain steady. This happens if your business grows while at the same time you work aggressively to control expenses. But when you borrow money to expand your business, some of your profit goes to pay interest. You do the work and the lender makes the money!

Equity Capital Disadvantages

You need to make sure that you and your new partners can get along together, share management responsibility and authority, and identify specific areas of expertise that don't cross over. The more money they invest, the more assertively the new partners will insist on the right to actively direct the course of the business.

The new investors might want more control over your business than you're willing to give up. Or they may undervalue your operation if you have a poor credit history, meaning you give up more for the same money.

> **Example:** An investor is willing to put money into the business even though you've had some credit problems in the past. But the new investor has some conditions:
>
> ▌ Weekly review of cash receipts and expenses.
>
> ▌ You must consult the new partner before you spend any money for anything other than normal operating expenses.

Another option might be that the partner will give you cash representing 25 percent of your equity, but in exchange, will demand *40 percent* of the business and its future profits.

Though these restrictions reduce your freedom, they might be necessary to get the cash you need. These conditions reflect the investor's higher risks associated with your credit history. Past bad credit has a price, and it's when you need money that you have to pay that price. A lender would require more collateral or higher interest under the same circumstances.

You might be lucky to find a potential partner or investor whose main interest is the results. They may see your skills as a perfect complement to theirs. They may have money and equipment to bring into the deal but need some of your skills and resources. They're not too concerned about your credit rating if they're confident that the two of you together will get the job done and make money.

You might need to change the form of your business from a sole proprietorship to a partnership or corporation when you bring in investors. The details of reorganizing a business are beyond the scope of this book, but these changes involve new requirements for tax reporting and planning, insurance, personal liability and estate planning.

For help in this task, you need to consult with an experienced tax accountant, and possibly with a tax attorney as well. The accountant should advise you on the benefits and consequences of changing your form of organization, in terms of taxation, reporting, and recordkeeping. For longer-term planning, retain a financial advisor with a lot of experience. In the best of all worlds, your accountant and financial advisor will work together to ensure that you undertake all aspects of your proposed change with a clear vision of the future.

Once you clearly understand the consequences of bringing in equity capital, you're ready for the next step. Figure 7-1 summarizes the pros and cons of equity capital.

Be Prepared to Sell Yourself

The first question a potential investor will ask you is, "Why should I put up money to go into business with you?" You need to prove several things:

▌ You're essential to the success of your development idea because of your skills and background.

Equity Capital Benefits	
You don't pay interest on money you receive from equity investors.	Investors receive their return on investment from the profits generated by your combined equity in the business, either through a salary or draw, or from a share of a project's profits.
Equity capital might be easier to get than a loan if your credit history is less than perfect.	Some equity partners may be willing to overlook a poor past credit record in exchange for a share in your expertise.
You add top-level management skills to your business with little added expense.	The new partner's draw is offset by money you formerly paid in salaries and professional fees.
You don't "pay back" investment capital the same way as a loan — through regularly scheduled payments.	You and your new partner both work to generate profits, so your total income increases enough to cover expenses and both draws.

Equity Capital Disadvantages	
You may lose some control over how you run your business.	People who own their own business tend to have healthy egos and strong opinions. That's good for a single owner, but in a partnership, such personalities can clash.
You give up part of your company's future profits	If you sell 35 percent of your company to an investor, that person gets 35 percent of all profits from then on.
You restrict your ability to raise equity capital in the future.	Suppose you've already sold 35 percent of your equity and you need to raise more cash. If you let go of more than 15 percent of what you have left, your equity partners will own more of your company than you do. They could team up and overrule you on important decisions. Or one could buy out the other. In either case, you'd become the minority owner of your company.
You'll need to reorganize your business.	Reorganization isn't expensive in terms of the mechanics, but it can be expensive if you don't anticipate the tax consequences. Federal and state laws change constantly, so these complex arrangements require the services of a professional and competent accountant, and perhaps an attorney as well.

Figure 7-1 Equity capital

▌ Your investor will make more money by joining forces with you than by investing in a competitor's business or competing with you.

Here are some arguments you can use when you approach sources for equity capital:

▌ "I've thoroughly researched this development idea and know there's an excellent market for the project." This is where your business plan comes into play. You can show a potential investor everything they need to know about your project and its likelihood for success.

▌ "By ourselves, neither of us can get the financing to develop a big project like this. Together, we'll have the strength to approach a lender." This argument makes sense when you and another contractor are both short of cash and can't get more by borrowing. In that situation, combining forces could make for one very strong company — and you might eliminate a direct competitor.

▌ "Your company and mine have skills that complement each other. We could both save a lot on overhead by working together."

The last statement describes the ideal situation where you and someone else go into business together and both of you have experience and skills the other one needs. A good match is where both sides benefit. You share the workload and you each save on consultants and subcontractors by combining the talents of your personnel.

By combining available funds, neither company has to repay a loan, and the combined operation makes more money than the individual owners did on their own. A combined business not only solves the financing problem, it may also eliminate a competitor for both partners.

For example, a general contractor might become partners with an engineering or estimating firm. Or you could team up with someone who has much more experience than you have in dealing with the local bureaucracy to work through zoning changes, conditional use permits and environmental compliance. That way, you'd save the cost of land use consultants and attorneys.

This works whenever both sides benefit. An engineering or estimating firm might be used to working for developers, but would like to enjoy an equity position. So you gain their expertise in dealing with zoning laws, building officials, or design. And the consulting firm gets part of the action in the development.

For details about how to present your case to an investor (or a lender), see Chapter 9.

How Do I Find Investors?

Networking is the key to finding money sources.

Once you decide to sell part of your equity, you have to find someone who wants to buy it. You could start by looking at your competitors.

The problem there is that if someone wants to get into the development business, and they have money to invest, they'll often want to do the job on their own. So be wary of approaching a strongly-financed competitor. This might only result in giving away your good ideas for someone else to take and run with.

You locate equity partners the same way that you find a lender. Check out the likely sources, ask questions, and follow up on every lead. Here are some resources:

- Newspaper classified or display ads

- Bankers and real estate agents

- Trade journals

- Responses to ads you place yourself

- Referrals from competitors, subcontractors, engineers or architects

- Other developers

Locating the right people when you need them is an important management skill. This is as true for finding equity capital sources or lenders as it is for recruiting the right managers and employees, consultants, and subcontractors. Networking is the key. Start by talking to everyone you know in town, including suppliers and competitors — especially those competitors who would add something of value to your operation if you went into a joint venture with them.

Is it an investor or a speculator?

Once you start looking for equity investors, you'll soon discover that they fall into the same two broad groups as developers themselves:

- The long-term investor who knows that development projects take time, and is willing to wait for the job to pay off.

- The speculator who is willing to invest — sometimes quite a lot of money — in your idea, provided they can make a big profit quickly by holding the land only until it's rezoned and goes up in value.

How do you tell the difference? If they talk a lot about potential profit, but don't have much of a track record as developers, the "developer" probably is a speculator. If they pay more money to land use consultants and attorneys than to construction companies, that's also a clue.

Check out developers who show an interest in your project. Review newspaper back issues and visit planning departments to find answers to these questions:

▌ Did they actually develop the land themselves or just buy and sell it for short-term profit?

▌ Did they keep their promises?

▌ What do the locals think about them?

As a starting point, ask for dates and places where the developers built in the past. Ask them for referrals to contractors or organizations they've worked with elsewhere.

If they ask you why you want the information, be honest and say that you want to check them out. You'll learn a lot from a developer's reaction to that. If they have nothing to hide, they'll gladly provide you with what you want. But if they hedge or get defensive, you probably have your answer to their developer status, and will be wise to look further for an equity partner.

Sometimes developers go into an area and make a lot of glowing promises in order to line up local support. They assure everyone that they'll buy up properties at premium prices, include nearby owners in a master plan, provide free public access areas, restore waterways, furnish public parks, or establish set-aside areas for environmental mitigation. But once the project is underway, some promises suddenly evaporate. It's important to know whether the individual you're talking to came through as promised, or was in the habit of deceiving the locals into supporting their plan.

Search automated news systems for the developer's name, then read the related newspaper articles. Check the minutes of local public hearings. You can get an extraordinary amount of information about a developer's track record in a day's worth of research.

Silent Partners

Some equity investors are interested only in the investment value, and don't want to be involved in the day-to-day operation of a business. That's often what people hope they'll find when they begin to look for equity capital. But that's not usually realistic. It's not often you can say "Give me the money and then stay out of the way." Few people will cheerfully turn over a bundle of cash without wanting some control over how you run the business. They want to be sure they'll get their money back, and make a good profit.

Remember that you're dealing with investors, not benefactors. So-called silent partners may be more flexible about *when* they're paid than an active working partner would be. But they'll be every bit as interested in *how much* they're paid.

Some people get into what they think is a silent partner arrangement, only to find out later that the "silent" partner turns out to be anything but silent. He might want regular reports about what you're doing. He might want to be consulted before you make major purchases or financial deci-

How silent is silent?

sions. He might want to make unexpected visits to your office to poke around and review what's going on. He might want to sit in on meetings, go with you to job sites, and order your employees around.

You'll probably consider these activities all unacceptable for a "silent" partner. But what can you do? You might end up in a very bad situation that could lead to disagreements and even lawsuits.

The answer is that you have to make absolutely certain before you make a deal that both sides know *exactly* what to expect. A person who isn't a developer or a contractor should invest their money in your company only if they have full confidence in you and your ability to manage the business. If they later want to help run the company, that's certain to cause friction.

You need to *define everyone's position up front.* You might spell out in the contract that the silent partner has no right to direct daily activities, but is entitled to a monthly financial statement. The investor might also be entitled to a quarterly dividend representing a share of profits, but not to a regular draw. For more on this, see "The Partnership Agreement" below.

Compensating Investors

You have a great development idea and you've found the perfect partner. Now you have to decide how you'll pay that partner. When you're in business alone, your budget includes your draw or salary. But when there's little or no money coming in, you're the last to be paid no matter how many hours you work. Now you have someone beside yourself to think about. Your new partner might not be so patient.

Investors expect a return on their investment, often beginning immediately. An equity partner in land development needs to understand that there will be no income until the development begins to sell. That could take several months, or even a couple of years. Make sure your partner realizes this from the beginning. *Make sure in writing!*

If you're lucky, your equity partner will be willing to wait to be paid until the job is finished. Of course, that's the best arrangement from your point of view. But if your partner *isn't* willing to wait, then you need to build into your development plan the draw or salary for your equity partner (and possibly yourself) during construction. You may have to borrow enough money for you and your partner to live on until the job is sold. This puts extra pressure on you to be sure the project stays on schedule.

If you have a nonparticipating equity partner — an investor who's willing to wait — you still need to agree about how and when that investor will be paid.

The Partnership Agreement

It's critically important that you thoroughly define every detail of your agreement with an equity investor. This contract is as important and binding as any loan contract and requires even more clarity. *Never* rely on verbal agreements or assumptions. The one certain thing in this business is that those will get you into trouble every time.

There are no standard forms for equity agreements because they're all different. But always be sure your agreement covers at least the following:

1. The precise amount to be invested.

2. Conditions of funding by the partner:

    ▌ Date and amount of payment (or multiple dates if funding will be paid in stages).

    ▌ Conditions under which payments are tied to job progress.

3. A clear definition of duties and responsibilities by each partner in daily operations, business decisions, scheduling, etc. Spell out in detail the partner's rights to hire employees, get loans, or make other management decisions. And be specific about what rights are excluded as well.

4. Payment arrangements — immediate or deferred. This section should define who is paid, when they're paid, formulas to calculate payments, and conditions of final settlement with everyone. Specify whether the equity partner is or is not entitled to annual dividends. Describe how profits will be calculated and distributed when the project is complete so that both sides know precisely what to expect. Will partners be paid immediately upon sale of the project? Or will payments be deferred according to construction phases or financing agreements with the ultimate buyer(s)?

    Specify that since payments to the equity partner represent a percentage of profits, those payments will be made *only* when profits are available. If you don't make money, the partner shouldn't expect to be paid. Any current period losses should be carried over and absorbed by future profits before compensation begins. This makes sense because you can't share profits that aren't there.

    One potential problem is that at the end of the quarter or year, profits might not always be available as cash. Those profits might be tied up in accounts receivable or inventory, or might have been used to pay down liabilities. For example, you might have contracted to rent a large part of the project, but haven't yet received money from the tenants. Base payments to partners only on cash *actually received*. Be sure you cover this in your equity agreement. Consider it when you prepare your cash flow projection as well.

Progress Report (monthly or quarterly)

Section I - Financial statements
- Balance Sheet
- Income Statement
- Statement of Cash Flows
- Accountant's or Auditor's statement

Section II - Budgets and forecasts
- Current forecast
- Forecast Variance report
- Current budget
- Budget Variance report
- Narrative section: explanation of significant variances

Section III - Discussions
- Project progress report
- Significant schedule changes and modifications
- Problem areas and contingency plans
- Financing discussion: status of loans and equity investments

Figure 7-2 Format for reporting to equity partner

5. Responsibility for later financing, whether through additional capital or through a lender, and who has the right to say yes or no to the decision.

   You need to spell out exactly how you'll get additional money down the line because interest payments come out of profits — yours and your investor's. The equity investor will be very interested in this.

6. Reporting to the equity partner:

   ▮ Progress reports — requirements and frequency.

   ▮ How often do you intend to provide your investor with financial statements?

   ▮ What do you need to report to your equity partner? Figure 7-2 is a list of some items you should definitely include.

   ▮ If, when, and how often does the partner have the right to review your books, or to ask for an independent audit?

   ▮ Is the partner entitled to see invoices, receipts, or contracts with subcontractors, lenders, or customers?

   ▮ Include conditions under which the partner has the right to approve major spending.

Incorporation

Forming a corporation and selling stock may sound easy. But it's harder to find investors for a privately-held company than for one that's listed publicly. Potential investors have a lot of choices about where to put their money, and a small construction company with high hopes may be far down on their list of preferences.

You might still consider incorporation as a way to raise investment capital, especially if you want to continue managing your day-to-day operation without anyone else's help or interference. When you're incorporated, investors hold the same position as they do in publicly-listed companies. As owners of common stock, they're silent partners with no right to manage daily operations.

You might ask friends or family to invest in a closely-held corporation, one with only a handful of stockholders who are often related to one another. But chances are you'll also try to sell stock elsewhere. A closely-held corporation is controlled by the stockholders, even when a minority holding of stock is owned by outsiders. This differs from a widely-held or publicly-listed corporation, which is controlled by an elected board of directors who then appoint officers to run the corporation.

Here's a word of caution, however. It's always a trip through shark-infested waters to involve family members and close friends in financial matters. Doing business with family members is full of potential trouble, which anyone who has sat through a session of Small Claims Court will attest. Family members don't have the same responses to borrowing, lending and investing as bankers have. I can't recommend investing with other family members unless you're experienced enough to give them confidence in your success. The best situation is one in which you and another family member are in business together already (perhaps running the family business that was passed down by your father) and with whom you have a good working relationship. You definitely want to avoid borrowing from relatives you don't like, your senile aunt, or any family members who are inexperienced but want to have a say in running the business.

Stockholders are entitled to a dividend if the board of directors declares one. The value of their stock rises or falls depending on several factors, which include:

▍ The company's profit

▍ The perception among investors as to the value of stock (which sometimes is related to potential future profits more than to current profits)

▍ The stockholders' understanding of the business the company transacts and what kind of future profit that might mean

▌ The nature of competition for the same development activity. If business is booming and many new projects are under construction, a well-capitalized and efficiently-run development company might be highly profitable. In that situation, chances are that stock values will rise.

In publicly-traded corporations, the annual stockholders' meeting includes votes on various issues. Shareholders can vote on only those matters described in the shareholder agreement. This is more true in widely-held companies, where no one person controls the voting stock.

Stockholders in a corporation vote for members of a board of directors. That board appoints officers to run the corporation. Minority shareholders usually don't have any rights to a direct voice in management. Set up your investor program along those same guidelines.

If you want to maintain controlling interest in your corporation, you have to hold onto at least 51 percent of the voting stock. But there are other creative ways to raise money without giving up control. For example, you might set up a class of stock that has no voting rights. But it's harder to sell such stock because investors usually want to be able to exercise their vote.

Setting up a corporation isn't a do-it-yourself job.

You need advice from a tax attorney to set up a corporation properly. It's dangerous to do it yourself because there are too many tax and legal questions to consider. Your corporation may come under the jurisdiction of the SEC (Securities and Exchange Commission), which means you have to comply with stringent recordkeeping and incredibly-complex reporting requirements to stockholders and tax agencies. To protect your long-term interests, especially when you sell stock to outsiders, *professional help is essential.*

A corporation is a legal entity and has the same civil responsibilities as a person. Violations of those responsibilities by the corporation could result in liability and, like a "natural person," the corporation can be sued.

The corporation exists as a vessel for one or more stockholders to operate with their assets working together. It's convenient because individual stockholders can buy and sell shares at will without disrupting the daily operations of the corporation. Stockholders don't own specific assets of the corporation like furniture, equipment, or cash. They own shares of the corporation in total. The corporation owns its assets directly.

Corporations report income and profit and pay taxes, just like individuals. But they're subject to different tax rates and use special forms to report their taxes. Tax liabilities may be higher or lower than for individual proprietorships or partnerships, depending on how they're structured. For example, one form of corporation is the S Corporation (previously called the Subchapter S Corporation), which operates and pays taxes like a partnership, but is legally structured like a corporation.

Many people believe that forming corporations protects them from personal liability. That isn't always true. If your corporation is sued and you're an officer, you'll probably be named individually in the suit, also.

Changing to a corporation can make things harder for you. For example, lenders might hesitate to lend money to your corporation unless you're willing to personally cosign for the loan. The lender might worry that if the corporation defaults on a loan, you'd refuse to honor it. Lenders know that sometimes happens.

Joint Ventures

A joint venture is a partnership or corporation formed strictly for one or more projects or for a limited time. Joint venture partners can be individuals, other partnerships, or corporations. You and your joint venture partners enjoy the benefits of equity partner investing, but don't have to permanently give up any ownership in your respective companies. Forming a joint venture solves the problems a lot of developers face:

▌ The need for cash and cooperation for a specified project only

▌ The desire to easily walk away from the partnership and retain full control of their company once the project is finished

This arrangement provides some separation from existing business operations, and combines the talent, experience and financial strength of two or more business owners.

> **Example:** You want to buy several hundred acres properly zoned for residential development, but you can't qualify for a loan. Another contractor in your town has the same problem. By forming a joint venture company, you create an entity that can qualify to borrow the money and to use existing capital to complete the project.

Each of you has different skills to contribute the job. Each partner stands to save thousands of dollars in subcontracting charges by having employees of the other business available.

The Silent Partner in a Joint Venture

You can also form a joint venture with a silent partner. You handle the entire project. The joint venture agreement spells out how the profits will be divided, how long the job will take, and when the money partner will be paid. As with any joint venture, it ends when the project is finished and sold.

This can be a winning deal for the money partner who's confident that you can manage the project successfully and make the best possible profit. They fund the project and you do the work. These equity partners are often willing to wait until the project is finished to collect their share.

The deal only works if everyone involved is rewarded afterwards. You have to be realistic. Recognize that anyone entering into this kind of contract is motivated by profit. The money partner might want a bigger share of the profit than you'll keep for yourself. And they might insist on being paid ahead of you if profits aren't as high as projected.

Types of Joint Venture

The choice between forming a joint venture as a partnership or a corporation depends on the preferences of the joint venture partners. Both sides might appreciate the value of joining forces for the specified project, but without wanting to join companies permanently. Some tax benefits might be available, such as deferral of profits if the joint venture uses the completed contract method. That means taxes are paid on profits only in the year that work is completed on a contract, even if the income is received (and costs and expenses paid) over many years.

If a joint venture organization plans to borrow money, it may be better off forming as a partnership. Lenders prefer partnerships because they can require the individual partners to commit personal assets as collateral to secure a loan. As we mentioned, it could be harder to collect from a corporation in the event of default.

But joint ventures still present complications to lenders because each partner has to be evaluated individually. Be sure that all joint venture participants have their own equity strength and excellent credit, so they'll be viewed favorably by a lender should the need arise.

Before you select a form of organization, consult your attorney and accountant about tax planning, capitalization of the joint venture, and the joint venture contract itself.

The Joint Venture Agreement

When you form a joint venture with one or more other companies, follow the same rules as for any partnership: Make sure that the agreement is clear to everyone involved. The agreement is a business contract, so it has to describe in detail all responsibilities and authority, and how profits are shared.

Whichever option you select to form a joint venture, it only works if everyone agrees on some basic points:

1. Who's in charge?

Who's the boss?
Define everyone's duties.
Who schedules the project?
Money matters.

One person has to be the undisputed project leader. Many joint ventures never get off the ground because the people involved can't get beyond this first step. You can't run a project by committee. This isn't a democracy where the majority rules — it's more like a constitutional monarchy. Someone has to have final authority to control day-to-day activities. This is usually the owner who has the largest share of responsibility and the most money at risk. This person is often the originator of the idea to begin with.

If your partner is a money partner only, you may need to furnish progress reports and financial statements. But be sure your partner understands that you're running the show and they have no authority to override your management decisions. The agreement should spell this out, but it can also limit your authority to make decisions without some controls. For example, you may agree that you won't spend money for capital assets or for costs above a specified dollar amount without prior approval from your new partner/investor.

2. Precisely who will do what?

This is where it helps if the joint venture partners have specialized skills that don't overlap. For example, if you're building a 200-house residential tract, you don't want four framing contractors as joint venture partners. If you're a framing contractor, you're better off with a foundation specialist, a plumber, an electrician, and a roofer, for example.

When two or more partners bring dissimilar but complementary skills to the joint venture (an ideal situation), the agreement should specify everyone's responsibilities.

3. Who manages the schedule?

This isn't always the project manager. It could be a supervisor or coordinating project foreman, assigned by mutual agreement between all joint venture partners. Just as the project manager has to be one person, day-to-day scheduling and supervision can't be shared. Efficient scheduling often makes the difference between profit and loss, so it's crucial in a big project to define who runs your overall project schedule.

4. Who invests how much?

You have to be very clear about the level of investment by each joint venture partner. Spell out the percentage of ownership and responsibility for each of the participants. If you'll rely entirely on cash supplied by your joint venture partner(s) rather than borrowing, be sure to distinguish clearly between financial responsibility and management responsibility *before any money changes hands.*

5. Who gets how much?

When the job is finished and begins to sell, how and when will you distribute the profits? If the project loses money, how is the loss divided? Who gets paid first, and by what formula? The joint venture agreement should cover all contingencies so that if profits are higher or lower than projections, it's absolutely clear to everyone how the deal is closed out.

It's the final division of profit or loss that often leads joint venture partners into court. When that happens, only one group profits — the lawyers. Lawsuits over business deals gone bad can last for years and end up costing far more than the amount in dispute. That whole mess can be avoided by taking great care to cover final distribution in complete detail before you sign the contract.

There can be many conditions in a joint venture agreement besides those just covered. A joint venture will be a smooth-running operation in which everyone wins if it's put together with the right people, and if everything is clearly spelled out in advance. But they too often get into trouble when agreements are unclear or not specific enough. Always have your accountant and lawyer prepare your joint venture agreement, then review it completely before you sign it. This agreement isn't recorded like a change in ownership of property. It's a contract, and as such it must comply completely with the law.

Participation

One kind of deal that works much like a partnership but is actually a form of joint venture is participation with a landowner. Under this arrangement, the seller reduces the price of the land to make it more affordable for you. In exchange, you agree to give the seller a percentage of your profits when you develop the land and sell it. The seller gets less for his land and effectively finances part of your development costs. This is also another way to "work with the seller" of land, as we discussed in Chapter 5.

The Debt-Equity Combination

We've talked so far about two alternatives: borrowing money or taking in equity partners. You don't have to choose between them. You can combine the two.

> **Example:** You create a joint venture partnership with a landowner on the condition that when the land is developed and sold, the owner gets a share of the profit. The owner pledges the land as collateral to borrow money for development and construction costs.

When a landowner isn't interested in developing the land himself, but sees the potential for your plan, this arrangement works well for both of you.

This also works if you want to develop an area owned by several different people. In fact, the joint venture equity-debt alternative might be the only practical way to proceed. Your other choice would be to buy out every owner. A creative approach involving debt-equity financing might solve the problem in a way that lets everyone make money.

You can propose the same options to several owners of small parcels of land as you would to a single owner:

- Offer cash for options or rights of first refusal, locking in a price you'll pay in the future.

- Agree to pay owners' master plan costs or legal expenses for rezoning or preparing Environmental Impact Statements, in exchange for options.

- Become part owner of the land in exchange for a share of future profits.

- Try to get the owners to carry contracts which stipulate deferred payments for purchase of the land.

A debt-equity combination also works when partners or joint venture participants combine their capital to buy land, then use their joint borrowing power to finance construction materials and business costs during development and before sale of the project.

Almost every business owner needs to raise cash eventually, whether it's to finance expansion or just to cover a short-term slow period, build inventory or buy new equipment. When you need to buy land *and* finance construction over months or years, the debt-equity combination is often the best answer to the question of how to raise the money you need.

"Divorcing" an Equity Partner

We can't leave the subject of investors without discussing the possibility that one day you'll want to regain total control of your company. The only way to reverse a partnership is to buy back the equity that you sold. Here's where you might run into a big problem. Few equity investment agreements specify terms under which original owners can buy out their investors — but they should. You might think that there's a fair market value for shares of your company, but it's rare that other owners will ever agree with you on that value.

It can be painful and expensive to get out of an equity agreement.

There's little doubt that you'll have to pay more than their original investment to buy out an equity investor. First, the investor wants a profit. And once you decide to buy back your equity, you and your investing partner may become adversaries. It's unlikely that the two sides cooperate willingly in that environment. The new part-owner might not be willing to give up their share, even at fair market value.

In that case, you have a tough decision to make. You can't force someone else to sell. But you probably could force liquidation of the entire business and then start over again with new investors. That's an alternative where both sides lose. It disrupts business, and often turns current profits into legal fees at the same time it delays continuation of business and future profits.

The best solution is to put a clause in the initial investment agreement providing that you have the right to buy out your investor(s) at current fair market value. Specify that the value will be set through binding arbitration, and that you'll pay no less than the initial investment amount plus an additional percentage that both sides agree upon — perhaps 5 to 15 percent or more.

So be wary when you choose equity capital as a way to raise money for your project. Like a marriage, it takes confidence and commitment to enter an equity agreement, and it can be painful and expensive to get out of it.

Chapter 8

Borrowing Guidelines

We've looked at two ways to launch a land development project when you don't have enough cash on hand: using other people's money (options, land trades and participation with the landowner) and equity capital through partners, investors or joint ventures. But still the most common source for development funding is from a lender.

Your project will take at least several months. And the project won't begin to produce income until near the end. Your other work will fall off as you devote your full attention to the demands of the new project. So you need money to cover your business and living expenses until your project starts to produce income. You need to know where to find the money, and in what kinds of packages you can find it.

How do you choose the right lender and qualify for a loan? First, we'll look at the business of "renting" money.

Money Basics

Renting money

Some business owners find the whole banking industry to be mysterious and confusing. But if you think about borrowing money as renting it, you'll understand better how loan officers evaluate applications, and how you can decide when and if to borrow.

Money is said to be "tight" when there's more demand for loans than there is money available. The result is always higher interest rates and tougher requirements for borrowers. It's just the opposite when a lot of money is available and demand is low. Interest rates drop. Lenders are out looking for business, so they loosen their restrictions.

You've probably heard the complaint, "Banks only lend money to you if you don't need it." There's some truth in this. Banks are concerned about risk. They want to lend money only to those who are most certain to pay it back on time. They're just like an equipment rental company who wants their trucks returned on time, clean and undamaged.

Money Availability

An equipment rental company has to maintain a stock of backhoes, tractors, trucks and other equipment to stay in business. It's the same with a bank. Money has to be available before they can lend it out and make more money. The success of your negotiations with a lender will depend a lot on the condition of the "money market" which governs how lenders operate.

Money is more plentiful for borrowers at some times than at others because the interest rate the lenders pay to the Federal Reserve system varies. Sometimes the lender's rate is too high for them to involve themselves with construction loans.

Money supply and demand

Money, like all traded commodities, responds to the forces of supply and demand. Federal law requires that banks and other lenders must set up reserves and keep on hand a specified amount of cash relative to the loans they grant. Banks can increase their reserves by borrowing money from the Federal Reserve. As their cash deposits increase, they can make more loans. But if the federal funds rate (the rate banks pay to borrow money) is too high, your local bank won't be able to offer a competitive rate. Then they might stay out of the lending business until the rate comes down. That's known as a "tight money" market.

At times the Fed (Federal Reserve Bank) purposely increases the amount of currency in circulation. The Fed operates a giant control mechanism, constantly adjusting the "temperature" of the economy by increasing or decreasing the money supply. So when the Fed wants to increase the supply, it lowers the federal funds rate, making it more attractive for banks to borrow. Then it's easier to get loans because banks and other lenders are actively looking for business.

Just as you pay more or less for materials depending on the supply and demand for those materials, banks raise or lower their interest rate according to the supply and demand market — for money.

Interest

The prime rate is the rate that lenders charge to their best customers.

The interest market is closely related to the money market and also reacts to actions by the Fed. Most lenders calculate interest rates based on the federal funds rate and the prime rate. The prime rate is the rate that lenders charge to their best (lowest risk) customers.

The prime rate varies with the federal funds rate. As the basic rate the banks pay (the federal funds rate) increases, so does the prime rate. Increases show up in mortgage loans and other parts of the money market.

Individual banks determine their own prime rate, but because all Federal Reserve banks are subject to the same rates, interest tends to be uniform between banks. The "prime rate" that's reported in the financial press is actually the typical or average rate charged by major institutions.

The interest market reacts to changes in supply and demand just like any other market. When more money is available, interest rates go down. When money is scarce, it costs more to borrow. Your project and your track record will also affect how much interest you pay. The higher the risk, the higher the interest.

Local Loan Sources

Don't forget that local lenders are highly sensitive to local conditions. Even when the national and international economic picture is rosy — money is plentiful and interest rates are low — local lenders will be cautious if the local economy is lagging. If large employers are leaving your area and unemployment is high, you might have a hard time getting a construction loan no matter how long you've been in the community or how good your reputation is.

But it can help if you know your banker personally and feel comfortable about banking on your friendship. The advantage you enjoy is related to the long-term and permanent nature of your business. If your operation is a local fixture, then a local banker knows you're not going to leave town suddenly and take off with their money. You have roots in the community and that means roots with the local lender as well. Even a cautious banker will overlook immediate economic indicators in favor of personal knowledge. You'll almost certainly do better with your loan request locally than with a branch of a large regional or national bank.

On the other hand, if the economy is healthy, new companies are coming to town, a building boom is underway, and everyone is optimistic about the future, your local lender will be eager to jump on the bandwagon.

Advantages and Disadvantages of Borrowing

There are several advantages of borrowing money for your project:

1. Limited obligation. You'll eventually pay off the debt without giving up any ownership in your company.

2. Repayment flexibility. You might opt to pay off the entire loan several months or a year from now. Or you can arrange for affordable repayments which you can make from current income by stretching the debt over many years.

3. Convenience. Loans are relatively easy to find. Equity partners may be more elusive. There are many lending institutions competing to lend money to qualified borrowers. But people who want to invest in exchange for part ownership in your company are harder to find unless your company is large enough to list publicly.

Dave found it very frustrating that the loan officer, despite the fact that finance was his business, simply couldn't understand that when there's no income coming in, it wasn't reasonable to expect the loan payment.

And of course, there are also disadvantages:

1. Repayment obligation. No matter what terms you arrange for repayment of your loan, you'll have to make those payments when they're due, without fail, even when business is slow or there's no money coming in.

2. Drain on working capital. Loan payments reduce the amount of cash you have available to pay employees and suppliers, not to mention yourself.

3. Interest reduces profits. Remember that it only makes sense to borrow when the use of borrowed money creates more profit than it costs in interest. Profitable debt is the only debt worth taking on.

Borrowing and Cash Flow

No matter whether you borrow money from a bank or get money from investors, cash flow management becomes important. You have to be sure there's money available from business operations to repay the loan, or to compensate your investors or partners.

Will cash flow and profits improve? If the answer is no, then why borrow at all?

We discussed cash flow while describing your business plan in Chapter 6, but let's review it briefly here. How does the infusion of new money affect your overall cash position? How much income will the additional cash generate? How much will you have to pay out (in interest and principal repayments, dividends, or salary) as a consequence of getting the money?

Will cash flow *and* profits improve? If the answer is no, then why borrow at all? The reason you want to expand your business is to make more money and improve the way your company operates. If borrowing reduces cash flow, that translates to lower profits and less control of your business.

> **Example:** You borrow $15,000 to buy a piece of equipment. You'll increase monthly income by $350 using the new equipment. But the loan payment is $500 per month, so your available cash drops by $150 per month over the term of the loan.

Maybe that's not quite what you had in mind. Let's try something else:

> **Example:** You bring in a partner and agree to a salary of $55,000 per year. You expect the money that partner invests, plus his special skills and experience, will increase your profit by $100,000 per year. In this case, annual cash flow improves by $45,000.

That's better. These simple examples demonstrate that bringing new money into a business can change cash flow in either direction. But it's worth repeating that even when profits increase, cash flow can be reduced by:

▌ Higher accounts receivable

▌ Increased inventory

▌ Paying off existing debts

▌ Buying capital assets

Cash flow problems may be especially severe when you raise money to buy land, because land improvements don't generate income right away. This isn't like remodeling or building a custom home for a client who makes progress payments throughout construction. You have to plan carefully how you'll manage cash flow during the months or years before your project starts producing income.

Interest Basics

The longer it takes to repay a loan, the more interest you pay. That's obvious. What may not be quite so obvious is *how much more*. Most people don't realize that when they finance their home over 30 years, they're paying almost three times more than the original cost of the house. That's because interest is always compounded and calculated on the outstanding balance of the loan. So in the first few years, very little of your payment goes toward paying down the loan — almost everything you pay is interest.

> **Example:** You borrow $100,000 and finance it over 30 years. The interest rate is 9 percent. Monthly payments are $804.63. Your first month's payment breaks down as $750.00 interest and $54.63 principal repayment. In the second month the payment breaks down as $749.59 interest and $55.04 principal.

As you can see, the loan balance goes down very slowly. At 9 percent over 30 years, you'd pay off only a quarter of the loan during the first 15 years. In this example, the total of all payments is $289,667, which is almost three times more than the original $100,000 loan.

This amortization schedule applies to home mortgage financing where the 30-year mortgage example is all too familiar to most people. But it also applies to developers, even though the loan term may be much shorter.

> **Example:** You borrow $100,000, but in this case the loan is due in five years. Interest is calculated on a 30-year schedule so the monthly payments are still $804.63 per month. But the unpaid balance of $95,880 is due after 60 months.

You structure the loan's due date to coincide with the planned completion and sale of your project, or to arrive at a time when you'll be able to refinance or extend the due date. Some lenders may charge higher interest for a short-term loan amortized over a longer period. Be sure you know exactly how much you're paying to borrow money.

Figure 8-1 is a table you can use to calculate what it will cost in total interest and what your monthly payments will be per thousand dollars for a loan of 5, 10, 15, 20, 25 and 30 years.

Years	5	10	15	20	25	30
	$245.60	$520.40	$827.00	$1,160.00	$1,520.00	$1,898.00

Example: For a loan of $80,000 amortized over 25 years, multiply the interest amount in the 25-year column by the loan amount:

$1,520 x 80 = $121,600

The total interest expense over 25 years will be $121,600. Add that to the loan amount, then divide by the total number of monthly payments to calculate your monthly payment:

$80,00 + $121,600 = $201,600
$201,600 ÷ 300 = $672 per month

Figure 8-1 Loan interest expense calculator

| Multiply the interest rate by the loan amount: | $80,000 x 9% = $7,200 |
| Divide the interest above by 12 (months): | $7,200 ÷ 12 = $600.00 |

Figure 8-2 Monthly interest-only calculation

Multiply the amount shown in the table by the total amount of the loan (in thousands) to find the total interest expense. The example is based on 9 percent interest, compounded monthly.

Types of Loans

For a development project that stretches over months or years, you'll probably deal with lenders more than once and for more than one type of loan. Different kinds of loans are better for different situations.

Mortgage or Acquisition Loans

This type of loan is a suitable option for buying land. Because you plan to develop and sell the land, this loan will probably be short-term. Either the loan will come up for renegotiation within a short time (three to five years), or you'll make a balloon payment of the entire unpaid balance. In either case, you can negotiate with the lender for payment options.

You may be able to work a deal where you make no payments at all during the loan term. In that case, interest accumulates and compounds until the due date, when you either pay the entire principal plus interest, or set up a new loan for the full amount.

You might arrange to pay only the interest — in effect, "rent" the money for a specified time. Interest is the same every month because the principal never goes down. You pay interest until the loan comes due and then you repay the entire loan balance. Figure 8-2 shows how to calculate the interest (which is also the monthly payment) for an interest-only loan.

The contract specifies conditions under which the lender can call the note and demand full payment. This may involve one of three possible scenarios:

1. A due date is set for some time in the future.

2. Demand with notice in advance is made at the lender's discretion.

3. The full amount is due immediately if you're late with a payment.

Remember that the lender will almost always require that you have some equity in the land. You may have to pay 30 percent or more as a down payment in order to get a mortgage. Don't expect the lender to finance the whole cost. That can happen, but it's a rare exception to the rule.

Construction Financing

This type of loan is designed to pay for the development phase in stages. You'll provide collateral for this type of loan, usually by pledging the land itself, assuming that you own the land free and clear. The lender will disburse funds according to a schedule as the project is developed.

This loan works much like a line of credit, but you'll often be subject to more supervision by the lender than for other kinds of loans. You may have to supply extensive documentation, such as copies of invoices and statements from suppliers, explanations about the use of materials, job schedules, comparisons between expenses and budgets, and regular financial statements. In this situation, the lender is acting more like an equity partner than a lender and they'll want to keep close tabs on your progress.

Bridge Loans

It would take very little slippage in your schedule to make it hard to pay off a loan that requires a balloon payment. It's unfortunate that in too many development projects, planned completion times are not met, and are pushed ahead time after time. That places a strain on all resources, particularly financial ones. You need to have a lender willing to work with you and grant bridge loans if necessary. There are so many factors beyond your control that can cause delays: subcontractor performance, supplier nondelivery, labor strikes, unexpected loss of key employees, illness, and a host of other causes. You should build a buffer into your schedule to help offset the unexpected delay, but chances are high that you'll need either a bridge loan or an extension, even in the best of plans.

> **Example:** Your land acquisition loan is payable in full in 36 months. Your development schedule predicts that you'll have sold enough units at the end of 30 months to cover the payment. But at the end of 30 months, the development is still about a year short of completion.

With a lot of money and time invested in the project, you face a default in six months unless you take immediate action. Both you and the lender have a lot invested in this project — and a bridge loan might solve the problem for both of you. This temporary financing will bridge the gap between now and the profit side of the job.

For this to work, it's essential that you've made *all* your payments so far on time. If the lender has had problems collecting from you in the past, they won't be eager to continue working with you in the future. They might simply demand payment and force you to find a different (and probably more expensive) source of financing.

As long as you've kept your end of the bargain, a bridge loan will be easier to get from your current lender. Bridge loans are common because lenders know that scheduling for lengthy projects is almost impossible to control precisely over the long term.

Permanent Financing

This loan can be for as little as two or three years, or for as long as 30. "Permanent" really describes a more stable interest rate and possibly the lack of the call demand feature usually associated with bridge financing. It's expected that you'll eventually sell the developed project and get out from under the debt.

You won't be able to get permanent financing to cover an entire project. Lenders will usually only finance 70 to 75 percent, depending on current market conditions. This is called the loan-to-value ratio. That means that for a project where you estimate construction costs at $400,000, the lender will probably offer you a maximum of $280,000. You'll have to come up with the rest.

Ask about your lender's loan-to-value ratio at the beginning of your negotiations. Federal regulations dictate the ratio for the kinds of loans that banks sell to a secondary market. Those loans are organized into pools (like mutual funds) and sold to investors. While construction loans don't often qualify for these pooled accounts in the same way as home mortgages do, lenders might apply the same loan-to-value ratio. Or the bank's policy may be to use a different ratio determined by its management for local construction loans.

If you own your land free and clear, the lender might add the land value to the construction costs, and then lend you a percentage of the total.

> **Example:** You want to finance a $400,000 project. The bank will lend 70 percent — $280,000. You need to come up with the difference of $120,000. You own the land free and clear and its current value is $75,000. The bank might add that to the loan, so you only have to come up with $45,000 in cash.

Lenders may not agree to consider the full value of the land in this formula if they fear that land values might fall.

Remember that lenders are driven by awareness of risk. They'll want to be sure you have enough stake in the project that their risk is reduced. The more of your own money you have invested in a project, the more fiercely you'll work to be sure that the project succeeds, and the less likely you are to walk away if things start to go badly.

Rules for Borrowing

There are rules for playing the money game. And like any game, you can't win unless you know the rules, and *follow* them. Your success in winning a lender over depends on how well you know the rules and how skilled you are at carrying them out.

A Checklist for Borrowing

Begin your checklist with answers to the same questions we asked at the beginning of this book:

1. Know how much you need.

2. Know how you'll use it.

3. Realize that the best way to get the money is to prove that you can pay it back.

Your business plan demonstrates the answers to those questions. The fact that money is *available* is never a good reason to borrow. The fact that money you borrow will produce more profit than it will cost in interest is the only valid reason to borrow.

Here's another rule: *Never borrow more than you need.*

Never borrow more than you need.

It's entirely possible that you'll qualify for a bigger loan than you actually need. Some lenders will even advise you to set up a "contingency" fund with the extra money. That might sound good, until you remember the principal of profitable borrowing. If you need $50,000 and it will cost you 8 percent, it makes no sense to borrow $75,000. That just means you'll spend more of your profits on interest.

If you pay off that 8 percent loan in a year, the extra $25,000 will cost you $2,000 plus compounding. That's a lot to pay for a contingency cushion sitting in your checkbook. Even if you have a checking account that pays interest, the interest you earn won't come close to covering the interest you'll pay out. You can place a portion of the "idle" money in CDs or other short-term investments, helping to reduce your interest cost somewhat. But follow these guidelines if you decide to do that:

1. Invest in relatively short-term CDs — 3 months, for example — so you'll be able to get the money out when you need it. You can always turn a matured CD around and reinvest it.

2. Always invest in insured accounts, like those in a bank. You can't afford to take risks (like investing in commodity futures or horse races), because this is money that's not yours to lose.

3. Remember that while your interest payments are tax deductible, interest income is taxable.

Who Are the Lenders?

When you need to borrow money, you'll probably think first of your small local bank or a branch of a larger banking chain. But these represent only a small part of the lending community.

Emerging Trends in Real Estate: 1999 lists the following breakdown of overall sources for debt financing of real estate in the United States (by percentage):

Commercial banks	39.8
Life insurance companies	15.0
Savings associations	10.0
Foreign investors	10.4
Pension funds	2.7
REITs	1.4
All other	20.7

Small Local Banks

Small local banks may not have the resources to finance a large development project. Their reserve requirements limit how much money they can lend, and sometimes even the types of loans they can grant.

A small bank with limited reserves might not be able to make portfolio loans (loans they keep rather than sell) on residential purchases, let alone development projects. Most small banks write loans and then resell them within three months. The buyers of those loans (known as the "secondary market") don't want to acquire anything except the safest and simplest loans — those for owner-occupied single-family homes, for example.

In those cases, the local bank processes loan applications, charges some up-front fees, pays out the money, then sells the loan to a government-sponsored mortgage pool. Two of the largest secondary market companies are the Federal National Mortgage Association (FNMA or "Fanny Mae") and the Government National Mortgage Association (GNMA or "Ginnie Mae").

A homeowner might not even know their loan has been handed off because the local bank continues to collect the money and impounds. But as a developer, you need to look beyond the community bank for the higher-risk and more specialized type of financing you need.

The only exception to this might be that your local bank could be a good source for short-term small loans or lines of credit. That's especially true if you have a long relationship (and a good reputation) with the bank.

Credit Unions

Your credit union might be willing to lend you money, though it's not as likely a source as other institutions, such as large commercial banks, savings and loan associations, and other major lenders.

Credit unions are often small, local, and have limited reserves compared to other lenders. They're protective of their members and unlikely to make high-risk loans. But they might offer limited credit lines or mortgages.

Consider your credit union as a potential source for backup emergency working capital through a line of credit in addition to your primary financing from another source.

Savings and Loans

Savings and Loans represent potentially-better loan sources than commercial banks because they face fewer regulatory restrictions over their lending activities. S&Ls are in the business of lending money. Banks are more likely to focus on serving their customers' personal banking needs. When they do write loans, they often do so only as a conduit to the secondary market.

Mortgage Brokers

Finding the right lender on your own isn't always easy because different institutions specialize in different financial products and have different requirements. The mortgage broker may be the best place to start in your quest for development financing. They specialize in matching lenders' products to borrowers' needs. A professional broker knows where the money is and can make the connections you need to tap into some of it. He or she does the research to identify the best lender for your type of project, makes the contacts, and then handles the paperwork for you.

Insurance companies are good sources of funds for certain development projects, but most developers don't know how to approach an insurance company directly. Many insurance companies aren't interested in lending money to finance development, so it's a waste of time to approach those. But a mortgage broker will know about the ones that are interested.

A mortgage broker insulates you somewhat from local economic considerations. Mortgage brokers search for loans by comparing current rates and terms for lenders all over the country rather than in a restricted geographic area. Local influences aren't as important today as in the past. Today you're not limited to your local or regional lending market — you can get financing anywhere. But local conditions are still among the factors a lender will consider when they review the feasibility of your project.

How do you find a mortgage broker? As with any other service professional, the best way is through referrals from other contractors and developers. You can find brokers listed under "Loans" or "Real Estate" in the classified telephone directory, or in the real estate section of your newspaper. An excellent way to comparison shop is on the Internet, where mortgage brokers are quite active.

While you're there, check out the National Association of Mortgage Brokers site (www.namb.org). It features lots of consumer information about their certification and state licensing requirements, business guidelines, and answers to common questions about mortgage brokers, what they do, and how they're paid.

Some mortgage brokers charge borrowers a fee, while others get their fee from the lending institutions that contract with them to find borrowers. Some brokers get a fee from both the client and the lender. In almost all cases (according to the NAMB), the broker isn't paid unless and until the loan closes. That gives them a lot of incentive to find the best possible match between lender and borrower.

You can see that borrowing money is more complicated than just walking into a bank, filling out a loan application, and walking out again with a check in hand. There are many sources, lots of options, and several strategies for sensible borrowing. To be a smart and successful borrower, you need to learn the basics, then find reputable professionals to help you get the biggest bang from your borrowed bucks.

Chapter 9

Convince Your Lender

You've done your homework on wise borrowing. You (or your mortgage broker) have picked out a suitable money source. Your next job is to persuade a lender to help finance your project.

The steps in this chapter apply whether you're approaching a financial institution or a prospective partner or investor. You may not fill out an application form when you seek investment capital, but otherwise the process is the same.

Before you present your application and business plan to a lender, ask yourself this:

If I were the lender, would I approve this loan?

Or when you're seeking investment capital, ask:

Would I find this project or company attractive?

From the investor's or lender's point of view, you'll only get a "yes" answer if you can communicate that you're a successful professional. You do that by presenting a clear and complete description of your development project that proves:

▌ There's a market for the project.

▌ The project is technically and politically feasible.

▌ You have the experience and resources to build the project successfully.

▌ You're financially secure and have a good credit history.

▌ You've minimized the risks that threaten your project.

You've written most of this evidence into your business plan. Now, just as with an employment interview, it's time to appear in person and sell yourself and your project. Figure 9-1 is a checklist you should use to make sure you've prepared yourself thoroughly for the interview. Go through it item by item, and consider if you can answer every question and provide the

Planning checklist

❑ Use past information and experience.

❑ Develop methods for documenting past activity.

❑ Design your plan as a working document — be prepared to amend it frequently.

❑ Use the business plan to monitor and control income, costs and expenses.

❑ Use the plan to convince lenders that:

    A. You are a worthwhile risk.

    B. You have thought through the problems.

    C. You are aware of what a lender needs to see.

    D. You know how to use numbers to make your case.

    E. You are well-organized.

❑ Make sure the plan shows — specifically — what you intend to achieve.

❑ Make sure your plan is tied together with goals.

❑ Follow your plan and use it as a control document.

❑ Revise the plan regularly.

Lender presentation checklist

❑ Make sure your plan works — the lender will want to know this.

❑ Describe your project clearly, simply, honestly.

❑ Include a discussion of the risks, not just potential profits. (Fill out the risk analysis worksheet to prepare for this discussion.

❑ Map out your profit plan.

❑ Prepare cash flow summaries to show that you can afford repayments.

❑ Demonstrate your management skill in the presentation.

❑ Anticipate the lender's questions and answer them in your proposal.

❑ Show a track record of using your plan to ensure success.

Market checklist

❑ Identify the specific demand and need for your project.

❑ Document your claims with marketing statistics.

❑ Demonstrate how recent past trends add to your arguments.

❑ Talk about the potential resistance to your ideas and how you will deal with it.

Figure 9-1 General checklist for the lender interview

❏ Tie together your marketing assumptions with dollars and sense:

    A. What will it cost per unit of construction?

    B. What is the likely sales price per unit?

    C. Identify the timing differences between construction and sale.

    D. Show how you have allowed for delay in the project.

    E. Identify likely problems and your contingency plan.

❏ Who is your target buyer? How will you reach that individual?

❏ What demographic information supports your project?

❏ What are the current market statistics and competition?

❏ Where does your project fit in the local scheme of things?

❏ What local benefits will be derived from your project?

    A. New employment.

    B. Community benefits.

    C. Environmental protection.

    D. Dedication of property as part of your project.

    E. New housing, workspace, or commercial benefits.

Project site checklist

❏ Show how and why the particular site was selected.

❏ What benefits does your site offer over others?

    A. Strategic location.

    B. Proximity to other services and facilities.

    C. Appropriate zoning.

    D. Community plan coordination with your project.

    E. Plans for development of roads and utilities to your site.

❏ What physical features make your site attractive for the project? What physical features are problematical, and how will you mitigate?

❏ What impacts of development might be seen by other property owners?

❏ How do you plan to mitigate those impacts?

❏ Have you budgeted for environmental review and process?

❏ Have you budgeted well enough for the cost of environmental mitigation?

❏ What extra costs will be involved to prepare the land before actual project construction will be possible (environmental buffers, grading, paving, utilities, etc.)?

Figure 9-1 General checklist for the lender interview (continued)

Goals checklist

❏ Have you listed a series of goals?

❏ Are those goals specific and realistic and are they project-related?

❏ Do your goals have deadlines?

❏ Do goals address essentials such as:

    A. Financing.

    B. Facilities and equipment.

    C. Personnel.

    D. Subcontractors and suppliers.

❏ Are goals based on specific assumptions?

❏ What is the documented basis for your assumptions?

❏ Can you demonstrate that goals can be reached based on information at hand?

❏ Do goals and assumptions address risk and propose contingency plans?

Forecast and budget checklist

❏ Are all of the numbers in the forecast and budget documented?

❏ Do your columns add up?

❏ Are your forecasts realistic and based on logical assumptions?

❏ Will your forecast and budget support your cash flow requirements?

❏ Is the forecast and budget easy to understand?

❏ Is the presentation cross-referenced and neat?

❏ Is the summary supported with all the necessary detail?

❏ Are you prepared to answer any financial question a lender might ask?

❏ If you're not comfortable talking about the numbers, are you prepared to visit your lender with your accountant?

Cash flow projection checklist

❏ Have you mapped out your cash flow requirements through the project period?

❏ Have you demonstrated a realistic use of cash?

❏ Does your plan include repayment of borrowed money, with interest?

❏ Are there shortfall periods?

❏ How will you deal with shortfalls? Does your plan include contingency plans?

❏ Have you mapped out the in-and-out and the timing of cash flow?

❏ Is the presentation format adequate to demonstrate your planning?

Figure 9-1 General checklist for the lender interview (continued)

documentation to back up your answer. If you can't, you're not ready for the interview.

Risk is always a lender's or investor's first concern, so let's begin with that.

Risk

Show the lender that you understand risk — from their point of view. Include in your written plan and in verbal discussions with lenders a discussion of why you're a "good risk." Let's look at the qualities that make you attractive to lenders and investors.

You Can Anticipate and Minimize Risk

You can't eliminate all risks ahead of time. But you can plan ways to respond when things go wrong. You need to demonstrate the following:

▌ You're aware of risks that can threaten your project.

▌ You have a plan to manage those risks.

Minimize lender restrictions by proving you're a good risk.

Business owners face risk every day — lost contracts, financial setbacks, accidents, bad weather — and your lender knows that. The lender's biggest fear is that you'll default on your loan. So be ready to argue successfully that you're aware of your risks and have taken steps to minimize, if not eliminate, them.

You know how insurance companies handle risk. If you're a bad risk, your premiums go up. It's the same with lenders and interest rates. Besides charging higher interest, a lender might also restrict the way they fund your loan. They might insist on paying loan proceeds in phases and require that you let them review your invoices and compare them to your project schedule as a condition of funding. They may even want to pay your suppliers directly. You could have a lender's representative looking over your shoulder throughout the project.

The way to avoid this is to convince the lender that you're a good risk. And the best way to prepare for that is to play a little "what if" game. Fold a sheet of lined paper in half vertically. On the left side, list all the awful things that could happen to damage (if not wreck) your well-planned project. For example:

▌ Fire in your office or warehouse

▌ Death of a key employee

▌ Natural disaster — earthquake, flood or storm

▌ Injury or damage caused by an employee

▌ Labor problems

▮ Changes in the political climate

▮ Interference by environmental agencies

▮ Zoning problems

▮ Permits withheld

▮ Lawsuits by no-growth advocates

▮ Your inexperience in certain areas (be specific)

▮ A drastic change in the local economy

▮ A jump in interest rates during the course of the project

▮ Running out of cash before the project produces income

Now, on the right side of the page, list your responses to these risks:

▮ Insurance you carry on property, vehicles, and key personnel (life, health, liability). Many insurers will cover specific business activities short-term. As a general rule, always insure against any loss you can't afford to cover yourself.

▮ Information you gathered in your land and political market studies. This will show if there's still information you need to find and include in your business plan.

▮ Contractual protection you've arranged against specific risks such as fixed interest rates on financing, or long-term labor agreements.

▮ Written commitments from local political bodies or agencies to support your project in advance. Comprehensive plans and neighborhood plans describe zoning and growth boundaries and have the power of contracts in case your project winds up in court.

Develop a response strategy to deal with each risk. Have a company disaster plan in place that covers everything from how to reach employees (or their families) in an emergency to procedures for backing up and storing computer files.

Maintain a list of resources you can enlist quickly if problems arise. Even if you don't presently use them, make initial contacts with an attorney, a land use planning consultant, an insurance and mortgage broker, alternate suppliers and a temp or employment agency or hiring hall. Then you'll already have a foot in the door if you suddenly need help from any of these sources.

Figure 9-2 is an example of the kinds of risks you might list. Doing this exercise will help prepare you to discuss risk with the lender or investor. Demonstrate that you know how lenders assess loan applications by anticipating their questions about steps you've taken to minimize risk.

Potential Risks	Planned Responses
Fire in office or warehouse	Proper insurance coverage
Death of a key employee	Key employee insurance
Natural disaster	Flood insurance
Injury or damage caused by employees	Casualty insurance
Labor problems	Negotiation/arbitration process
Changes in the political climate	Written commitments regarding zoning
Interference from environmental agencies	Select land carefully to minimize
Zoning problems	Documentation in county plan
Permits withheld	Hire a land use attorney
Lawsuits by no-growth advocates	Negotiation/legal countersuits
Negative experiences	Watch out for same problems
Drastic changes in the local economy	Cautious forecasting — mitigate
Jump in interest rates	Lock in today's rates by contract
Cash flow problems	Better planning — worst case scenario

Figure 9-2 Risk analysis worksheet

The "Good Risk" Financial Profile

What are the elements that make you a good financial risk? A good risk has consistent, positive behavior to report. Show that you have a clean track record of impeccable credit history for at least the past two years.

Even if *you* think your credit history is perfect, check to see what the credit bureaus report. That's what your lender will do to verify what you write on your loan application. It could be that six years ago a charge card payment of $10 was posted a day late because of a holiday. You may not remember this, but the credit bureau will, and it'll be on your report. Don't let the lender discover this for you. For current copies of your credit report, telephone, write, or e-mail the three national credit reporting bureaus:

▮ Experian (formerly TRW) toll-free 1-888-397-3742, e-mail www.experian.com

▮ Equifax toll-free 1-800-685-1111, e-mail www.equifax.com

▮ Trans Union, PO Box 390, Springfield PA 19064-0390, e-mail www.tuc.com

Credit reports cost around $30. But you can get a free copy from any agency whose report led to a decision to deny you credit in the past 30 days.

If you find an error in a credit bureau report, notify the credit agency in writing of the actual circumstances and demand a correction to your file. If you can't get it resolved before you apply for the loan, include a copy of that letter with your loan application.

If your credit history is poor or inconsistent, there's nothing you can do to change that now. What you *can* do is demonstrate to the lender that your management techniques have changed and your credit record has improved.

Reveal the precise nature of any past credit problem. Then describe the steps you took to overcome it. If a creditor has won a suit against you for a default in payments, or you've filed bankruptcy in the past, provide more information, but make it brief. Don't blame past problems on others or claim that those problems were beyond your control. That makes people suspect that you don't accept responsibility. Instead, acknowledge your mistakes even if outside influences contributed to your situation.

Lenders understand that you're human and that humans make mistakes. Even with a spotty credit history, it doesn't necessarily mean your loan application will be denied. The lender is looking for a *pattern*, not an excuse to deny your application.

Here are some factors that are evidence of good financial risk from the lender's point of view:

▮ Living in the same place longer than a few months at a time

▮ Steady, long-term employment or business history

▮ Steady, consistent income

▮ Loans and bills paid on time

▮ Limited use of revolving credit accounts

▮ No past defaults, judgments or bankruptcies

▮ No evictions or past civil or criminal convictions

▮ Efficient management of business accounts, payroll, and tax deposits

▮ Little or no use of short-term borrowing to manage cash flow

Notice that the recurring theme in this list is *consistency*.

Expertise

Consider including your personal résumé, either as part of your business plan, the cover letter, or as an attachment. Your lender or investor may know little or nothing about your past history or experience, but a brief achievement-oriented résumé will fill in the blanks for them.

Your résumé should describe your areas of expertise and major accomplishments, rather than simply listing where you worked, when you worked there (and how long), and what position you held. Focus on financial successes and project management skills — past projects you completed on time and within budget — whether as a business owner or an employee.

If you're working with partners (including joint ventures), furnish résumés for all the key players. Also mention the outstanding talents and achievements of your associates, whether partners or employees, especially if they've been publicly recognized either through media publicity or awards from civic or professional organizations. Lenders and equity capitalists want to know their money is in the hands of a team with a proven track record for success in construction or development.

Feasibility

Your lender or investor may bring up the subject of a feasibility study. This might lead to some confusion, so let's define what we mean.

As far as the lender is concerned, they view feasibility in terms of your market, the prospect that you'll repay your loan in full and on time, and their "sense" of the project itself. In other words, is it feasible that your project will make a healthy profit?

But the term "feasibility study" can also refer to a technical document that covers all aspects of a project related to getting permits, passing environmental review, and complying with all local, state and federal government regulations. Your planning department, zoning commission, environmental protection agency or pollution control district may require copies of this technical feasibility study.

Preparing this may require help from land use consultants, attorneys and technical experts such as geologists, engineers, ecologists, utilities managers, and estimators. The feasibility study contains soils, design, environmental and engineering analyses, maps (especially if wetlands or habitats are involved), cost estimates, and an Environmental Impact Statement if required. Federal, state and local jurisdictions might each demand that you fulfill their own special requirements.

You probably won't be expected to furnish this type of feasibility study as a direct requirement for financing. The lender's main interest is in feasibility as described in your business plan and market studies — financial rather than technical feasibility. But you need to be able to tell your loan officer that your project will meet those technical feasibility requirements. Here's where it's reasonable to hire a land use consultant to prepare a preliminary summary indicating that your project is likely to qualify under prevailing laws and regulations. It wouldn't be practical to do a full-blown feasibility study before your loan is approved. Nor should you have to become an expert on technical feasibility yourself.

Your lender might want to see some technical confirmation that your plan will go through. And satisfying the lender's concerns will cost money.

> **Example:** You have a target piece of land for your project. The lender is satisfied with your financial strength and the marketing prospects for your development. But the loan officer has some doubts about the plan itself and wants assurance that it will pass environmental review, that there won't be any violations of wetlands protective regulations, and that soils analysis confirms that the site will support your development without expensive mitigation.

It would be risky to pay for feasibility studies on land you don't own — but you don't want to buy land that's not feasible for your project. So you'll run into some trick timing here. I recommend that you find a good real estate agent who understands how land development processes work and can help protect your interests.

You can try to persuade the seller to accept your offer contingent upon loan approval as a condition of sale, then pay for only the feasibility studies the lender requires. The others can wait. Otherwise you might spend too much money on fees and consultants before you're even sure you can buy the land.

The Project Will Sell

Be sure you've double-checked and memorized all the important facts and numbers in your market study before you present it to your lender. This attachment to your business plan summarizes your research about your prospective clients and describes how you intend to turn those clients into buyers or tenants.

This may be the key part of your presentation in terms of reducing your lender's concerns about risk. They want to be sure this project will sell at a hefty profit once it's built. You need to emphasize how thoroughly you studied the market and that you found answers that prove your plan is built on a solid foundation of valid financial expectations. The way to do that is to discuss your market plan clearly and confidently, without hesitation.

Your Approach

In today's world of electronic communication, it's easy to forget the importance of personal contact. Don't rely entirely on the convenience of the telephone, fax or e-mail. When it comes to borrowing money, the impression you make in a face-to-face meeting is just as important as the quality of your written material. Give the loan officer a chance to connect your face to your name and your project.

Use an approach that fits your situation. A casual approach might work best if you live in the town where you were raised and you're applying to a banker you knew in high school. Expect a more formal atmosphere at a large bank where you don't know anyone. Dress up. If you need a cheering section to bolster your confidence, take your accountant along to back you up or field questions.

Here are some guidelines for meeting a lender:

▌ Call ahead to learn whether the lender requires that you submit an application form. If so, get a copy so you can fill it out and sign it ahead of time. And remember, neatness *does* count. Type the form or print neatly in ink. The lender's first impression is important. Remember that the person who first reviews your application might also be the one who ultimately decides whether to approve or refuse your loan. Don't let a sloppy loan application tip the scales against you. (Be sure to keep a copy of the completed application for yourself.)

▌ Make an appointment and be on time.

▌ Have written materials well organized, labeled, and neatly packaged. Bring a copy for yourself (and anyone who accompanies you). Highlight and bookmark your copy so you can easily turn to relevant sections during your presentation.

▌ Bring along any visual aids you have available — anything that will help the lender visualize your dream. That could include floor plans, elevations, models or architect's drawings. They could provide the last nudge needed to sway the lender in your favor, especially if other builders have approached them with a similar project.

▌ Follow your appointment with a phone call the next day. Even if you have to leave a voice mail message, at least say, "I appreciated meeting with you yesterday. I'm calling to be sure you have everything you need. If you need anything more, please call me at (give your phone number). Thanks again. I look forward to hearing from you."

What the Lender Wants

It's hard to guess what a lender might request from you. But you're more likely to be prepared if you remember what you've learned about how lenders evaluate risk. Your job is to anticipate the lender's questions as best you can and provide answers *before* the lender asks for them.

For example, if the loan application doesn't specifically require tax returns, bring copies for the last two years anyway. Furnish these whether your business is a proprietorship, a partnership or a corporation. Bring copies the lender can keep. Don't expect bank personnel to make copies for you.

Disclose anything about your business that might interest the lender. Tell them if you plan to operate the project as a joint venture, or if you intend to restructure your business to form a corporation or partnership. Take the documents which support these changes with you to the bank.

The Loan Application

When you go into an institution to hand over a loan application, or when you fill out an application for a mortgage broker, you'll see that the questions fall into two general classifications: personal and financial.

Application forms typically require the following information about you (and your spouse if you're married):

▌ Name, residence address, mailing address, and phone number

▌ Length of time you've lived at your current address and whether you own or rent the property

▌ Identification, such as marital status, social security number, driver's license number, and mother's maiden name (for security purposes if a checking account is involved)

▌ Employment (including gross income), and employment history for the past 10 years

▌ Annual expenses for house payments, taxes, outstanding loans, alimony, or child support

▌ Life insurance amounts

The financial part of the application is nothing more than a personal balance sheet. You're asked to list your assets (things you own), your liabilities (money you owe), and your net worth (assets minus liabilities).

Don't mix business and personal information on the loan application. But include your business net worth as a line item on your personal balance sheet. Then attach a copy of your business balance sheet, or refer to the

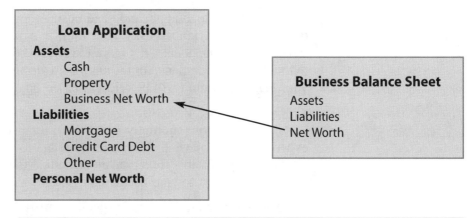

Figure 9-3 Your loan application

financial statements section of your business plan. Figure 9-3 shows how this works.

Keep the loan application clean and simple. Use only one line for each item and use attachments (schedules) to show the details. For example, if you have outstanding balances on several credit cards, attach a schedule listing each account with its balance and monthly payment. Include only the totals on the application as a one-line liability, with the notation, "Schedule Attached."

Here are some more tips:

▌ *Disclose everything* — even the bad stuff. The bank will learn the truth when it gets your credit report anyway, so you gain no advantage by leaving out negative information. The lender will be suspicious of your entire loan package if they find that even a small part of it isn't complete and honest.

▌ *Don't exaggerate* — stick to the truth. Don't overvalue personal assets, for example. If your house is worth $125,000, don't show its value as $200,000. Be realistic. And again, remember that the lender will verify everything you report.

Waiting for the Answer

The toughest part during the days following your interview with a lender or investor is waiting for a decision. But no matter how carefully you've tried to cover all the bases, the lender may have questions. It's a *good* sign if the lender asks questions. If they're evasive and don't want to talk to you, but promise to notify you by mail within a few days, that could be a bad sign.

Even the best loan application and business plan is likely to spark questions. When the lender asks questions, it's usually not because your information is inadequate. It's more likely to be that they aren't sure where to look in your documents for the answers. Questions reduce the chance that your loan application will be rejected based on an error or misunderstanding.

Answer questions promptly and with assurance. Remember, *you're* the expert on this project. If the questions relate to your financial affairs and you're not comfortably fluent in "money talk," ask for the questions in writing and refer them to your accountant.

Some questions may relate to specific parts of your business plan.

> **Example:** The lender views your cash flow projection as "tight" and based on an overly-optimistic schedule and outcome. They want more information about how you plan to manage cash during periods when expenses are especially high.

Prepare for this question by making sure that your cash flow projections are extremely accurate, that they have some built-in flexibility, and that you have a backup plan you can describe "off the top of your head."

Your backup could include delaying a scheduled capital purchase, using a short-term line of credit, reducing the time required for other plan elements, or modifying the entire plan based on circumstances at the time.

It's best to include backup alternatives in your business plan. That forces you to think about possible unexpected events, *and* shows the lender that you know that things sometimes don't work out according to schedule.

Apply the same kind of contingency planning to expense budgets and income forecasts. You anticipate questions by building the answers into your plan.

Admit to the lender that your plan is based on the best information you have today — but that like all plans, it's just a guideline, subject to change as circumstances change. That's plain and honest.

It's our lack of certainty about the future that makes planning interesting as well as dangerous, and adds the element of risk to all tough decisions. But it's wise and thorough planning that minimizes the risk.

What If You're Turned Down?

Business owners make tough decisions every day. You made one when you decided to expand into land development. Many things can go wrong, and you go into any plan knowing that. That's part of being in business for yourself.

Lenders sometimes make mistakes.

The lender's in the same position. They make tough business decisions both when they accept loan applications and when they reject them. There's no way to know for sure which applicants are good risks, so lenders have to calculate the odds and go with the tactics that usually work. They also sometimes make mistakes.

If your loan application is rejected, follow these steps:

1. Remain calm. You need answers now, but you'll have less chance of getting them if you go bristling down to the bank in a huff. Take time to cool off and reflect. The decision wasn't personal. You'll find a solution. Keep these thoughts in mind before you take the next step.

2. Make an appointment to meet with the loan officer again. Ask for specific reasons why your application was turned down. Discuss each issue as it comes up. Make careful notes of the lender's remarks. Clarify anything you suspect the lender may have misunderstood.

3. Revise your loan package to include any information you left out, or add documents that will help refute the lender's reasons for turning you down. Show evidence to correct information supplied in error by a credit reporting service.

4. If you're rejected because of a misunderstanding or incomplete information and not because of credit problems, you should firmly ask the lender to reconsider once you supply what's needed.

5. Bring in more cash if that will help. Some lenders refuse loans because they believe the borrower simply doesn't have enough financial strength. You might be able to get money from someone in your family and bring them into the business as an equity partner. This looks better on the books, even if you'll pay your relative back later without interest or profit. But be alert to the problems that may come up when you borrow from family members. You don't want it to look like you're attempting to deceive the lender, and you also don't want problems with your relatives themselves. If they're listed as equity partners, does that mean they're liable if the company is sued? Consult an attorney to be sure that loans from family members are set up properly and everyone is protected, including you.

6. Find a different lender and start over. Maybe nothing you say or do will persuade the present lender in your favor. Sometimes you have to shop around before you find someone who's willing to work with you on your project.

Having learned his loan application had been denied, Dave follows the advice
in the book to stay calm and to make an appointment to see the loan
officer to clarify anything he may have misunderstood.

Remember that lenders make money by lending money. Like any business, they need customers. The interest you pay is the lender's profit. If you have generally good credit and equity in your company, you should be able to find a lender to finance your project.

Here's some final advice about dealing with lenders: Lenders may require up-front loan application and processing fees, credit reports or appraisals. These may cost up to several hundred dollars. Ask for your money back if you've prepaid any fees and the lender refuses your application without a specific and valid reason. If your rejection was based on an error rather than on an actual flaw in your credit or financial condition, the lender shouldn't keep your application fee.

Your experience in applying for and getting a loan will vary depending on your project and your lender. In this chapter, we've considered the basic rules for interacting with loan officers and committees, and presenting yourself and your project convincingly. As long as you believe in the project and in your ability to manage the financing, you're prepared to take the next step — getting the money and going to work.

Chapter 10

Get on With the Project

Hooray! You've got the money. Now you're ready to turn your dream into reality. Here's some final advice about how to make sure your project stays on track, that you're able to repay your lender or investor, and most important, that you make money.

Transition isn't easy. It doesn't matter whether you move into a new field (like land development) or simply expand your existing activities. Problems come up whenever you make major changes in your business. But it isn't the problems themselves — it's the way you handle them that can make or break you. The secret is to recognize trouble as soon as it rears its ugly head so you can react quickly.

Good management means solving problems before they become disasters.

Good management isn't just planning ahead to anticipate every problem. It's the ability to solve problems before they turn into disasters. Your most important job during transition is to steer your business successfully around the obstacles that come with growth.

You created your business plan as a blueprint to reach your goal and create a successful project. Now it's time to use the plan for its next most important purpose — monitoring your success.

Stay Focused

When you started thinking about your project, you clearly visualized the end result. The steps you've already taken forced you to consider every detail that will go into the job. Stick to your plan, and your prospects for success improve dramatically. But your plan has to work as well in the field as it does on paper. The rest of this chapter describes how to be sure it does — and how to change it if it doesn't.

Here's a list of things to do regularly over the course of your project to be sure you're staying on track:

1. Set up a procedure for your bookkeeper to report a monthly comparison of direct costs and overhead expenses to budget estimates. Adjust the budget whenever discrepancies appear.

2. Take another look at market conditions to be sure they haven't changed significantly since you wrote your original market study. Do this quarterly.

3. Update your project schedule weekly (if not daily). Pay special attention to the "critical path" items which would delay steps that can't start until an earlier step is finished.

4. Clamp down on overhead expenses. Charge your office manager with responsibility for reviewing overhead accounts each month with the goal of reducing overhead as much as possible.

5. Keep a close eye on direct costs, especially labor.

6. Monitor equipment usage to be sure it's "paying its way."

7. Review cash flow each month against your projections.

Let's start at the beginning of the list. The first thing to do is to set up procedures for making regular comparisons between what you expected to spend and what you actually spent. One reason you made a budget was so you could monitor results each month and spot trends as they develop. This is easy to do. First, break each budget item into monthly components. Use a format like the one in Figure 10-1.

Write the month's total in the "actual" column of each expense line. Copy the amount from your budget for that category in the "budget" line. Calculate the differences for the month and for the year to date. The last column is important because it helps you see trends which might seem insignificant in a month-by-month comparison, but which could get out of hand over several months.

Define significant budget vs. actual differences ahead of time.

Investigate differences between your budgeted and actual expenses only if those differences are significant, based on rules you set up ahead of time. For example, you might define "significant" as any amount over $100, or 5 percent or more of the total budget amount. That way you won't waste a lot of time chasing down relatively small variances.

The rules don't have to be the same for all budget line items, and you can change them over time. You can add a column to your comparison chart that shows the validation rules.

Your expense analysis will be much more accurate if you make sure that all payments are consistently coded and assigned to the proper bookkeeping accounts. It's easy to post expenses to the wrong account if your definitions aren't clear or specific enough. For example:

▌ Postage: Separate this from Office Supplies, or use a sub-account.

▌ Business cards: These might be a sub-category under Promotion, Office Supplies, or Printing.

Description	Actual	Budget	Monthly Difference	YTD Difference
(Budget line item)	xx.xx	xx.xx	xx.xx	xx.xx

Figure 10-1 Analyze budget vs. actual costs

▌ Vehicle maintenance: Your car service might go under Automotive Expense, but you'd charge routine maintenance of your backhoe to direct costs for a specific job.

An efficient set of accounting books is consistent, simple for your bookkeeper to use, and easy to analyze. Spend a few minutes each week reviewing payment codes in your check stubs or disbursements journal before they're posted to the individual accounts. It's better to find mistakes — and you will — when it's easy to correct them.

Check Your Assumptions and Goals

These are assumptions that relate to your project goals, not the ones you projected when you filled out your budget. Review your Goals and Assumptions Worksheets at least once each quarter to be sure your initial assumptions are still valid. Return to your market studies and update critical information if you suspect recent events may affect the success of your project.

▌ Has there been a change (either way) in the spread between asking and selling prices?

▌ If you're building residences, do population and employment numbers and trends remain steady and consistent with your predictions?

▌ If yours is a commercial or industrial project, will recent local events affect the labor pool or customer base?

▌ Were your assumptions about your competitors flawed? Might their present activities affect your profit?

This is not the time to hide from your lender. That dooms your chance for help later if things get really tough.

All kinds of things — from natural disasters to announced business mergers, relocations or shutdowns — can cause changes in your market study predictions. These can significantly reduce demand for your project if it won't be finished for a year or more.

The key here is to recognize market changes which affect your assumptions as soon as they occur, and to react quickly. This is *not* the time to hide from your lender. That's a mistake because it dooms your chance for any cooperative teamwork later if things get *really* tough.

Visit your lender as soon as you see trouble on the horizon. Present your ideas for solving the problem, whether they be to stop work temporarily, to reduce the size of your project, or to stretch out the timing so your units hit the market after its cycle starts up again. If you show your determination to find a solution while the problem is still fixable, your lender may be willing to suspend repayment (letting interest accumulate), or work with you in other ways to help you weather the storm. Remember, they have an investment to protect also. They'd rather be paid later than not all!

The Project Schedule

Remember that goals are set up to reflect deadlines as well as actions. When you miss a deadline, that can foul up everything that comes after. Stay in close touch with your project manager and ask questions about all scheduled events:

▌ Did expected deliveries arrive on time?

▌ Are work crews and subcontractors performing according to expectations?

▌ Has the weather caused any serious production setbacks?

Don't wait until any of these events cause delays of several days or weeks before you're aware of them. The time to react to slips in the schedule is *immediately*.

Forecast and Budget

Compare actual payments to your budget every month, *without fail*. If you don't, then preparing the budget was a waste of time. When you find a variance, identify the cause immediately. Only then will you know how to fix it.

Overhead Expenses

Review your budget assumptions to see if they're still true. If they're not, then find answers to these questions:

▌ How should I change the budget?

▌ How do I need to change the monthly budgets and cash flow projections from here on?

Remember that your budget is a tool, not a rigid plan that can't be changed.

Look again at the evidence you used when you set up your budget accounts to see if they're still valid. Budgeting is an ongoing discovery process. Things that made sense several months ago might be out of date now. You may have to abandon some original assumptions and replace them with current facts. Be alert, and especially, be flexible.

Here are examples of some steps to take when a budget item goes out of line:

▌ If you've let employees buy supplies and equipment without prior approval in the past, stop now! Begin a policy to require approval of a requisition before anyone buys office supplies or small tools. Assign someone in your office to maintain the supply inventory and fill day-to-day requests. And don't let employees use the company postage meter for personal mail without reimbursement.

▌ Set up a telephone log to record long distance or toll calls and demand that employees reimburse the company for personal calls. Your goal is to prevent expense overruns, and that might require efficient control systems that produce some increase in procedures and paperwork.

If you discover "leaks" in your expense forecast that prove your budget is wrong, revise it immediately. It never makes sense to stick with a budget that's obviously unrealistic, especially once you spot the problems. Attack each flawed assumption as soon as you discover it so you can make small changes without having to revise the entire budget. Remember that your budget is a tool, not a rigid plan that can't be changed for an entire year or the course of the project.

Your budget becomes a valuable profit center in its own right. Most people keep a close eye on the big picture — sales revenue and direct costs — but they forget to watch the small stuff. Remember that every dollar you cut in overhead becomes a dollar more in profit. That's the essential value of budgeting, and it's why we refer to the budgeting process as a "profit center." The more care you take in monitoring and controlling expenses, the more money you'll make.

Direct Costs

The main thing to look for when you analyze direct costs is a variation in the percentages as compared to sales (or in the case of land development, expected sales). The ratio between direct costs and sales should remain fairly consistent.

The biggest source of variances in direct costs is for labor. Here are some things to watch for that will alert you if your workers are costing you more than they should:

▌ Overuse of highly-paid workers for lower-level work. Don't pay skilled trades to do simple labor.

▌ Excessive idle time due to poor management by supervisors, delays in material deliveries, or poor scheduling of inspections. Include a "remarks" column on your timecards for workers to record reasons for idle time.

▌ Poor payroll practices. You're better off keeping your crews a bit lean than having more people on the books than you need. It's usually worth it to deal with the inconvenience of hiring and laying off people week to week.

▌ Improper mix between direct labor and subcontracting. It's tricky to figure out which is more efficient. If you know you'll have enough work over the next three months for a crew of 12 finish carpenters, it makes sense to put them on the payroll. But later in the project, you could be better off paying a subcontractor to occasionally install custom lighting fixtures for buyers of your units instead of interrupting your electricians' regular work flow.

Excessive direct costs often show up dramatically in big dollar amounts. That's why it's especially important to monitor those carefully with an eye to preventing them, instead of trying to cut back after you discover a problem. It's hard to recover from a big overrun in direct costs that's been going on for a month or more.

Keep a special eye on material costs. Compare current prices to your takeoffs and estimates. If prices are on an upswing, you might consider buying further ahead of need to protect yourself from higher costs in the future.

Capital Assets

It isn't enough to know whether you're "within the budget" on each expense category. There are more subtle things you have to look for. For example, some expenses may "drop out" and be replaced by other, sometimes higher ones, during the project. It takes a sharp eye to see when that happens, and constant attention to detail to adjust accordingly. This kind of thing happens most frequently where trucks and heavy equipment are concerned.

> **Example:** Maintenance and ongoing repairs on your heavy-duty truck exceed budget to the point where it makes more sense to sell or trade it for a new one. Routine maintenance and repairs for the new truck will drop dramatically, but you'll have the added outright cost or payment expense for that new vehicle. Adjust your budget to reflect that.

When is it time to replace a piece of major equipment? Just track your repair costs, using a sub-account for each truck or machine to see when repair bills start climbing. And remember that it isn't just repairs that cost you money — idle time does too. Keep a usage log for heavy equipment where you can easily spot increasing idle time caused by breakdowns and repairs.

When you think about alternatives to buying or leasing new equipment, also consider the relative cost to hire a subcontractor with the equipment you need, just when you need it. That way you can let someone else worry about downtime, maintenance and repairs.

Cash Flow Projection

You might need to change the month-to-month mix in your budget based on what you're seeing in actual results in cash flow. Carefully compare cash flow against your projection each month. Take immediate steps to stop a trend that reveals an unexpected decline. Those steps all relate to control of working capital, and require that you pay close attention to the accounts that affect available cash.

Accounts Receivable

Lots of businesses go broke even though they're owed a lot of money. If you're still doing small jobs left from before you began your expansion or development project, pay special attention to your accounts receivable.

▌ Don't let outstanding short-term accounts receivable age beyond 30 days.

▌ Be aggressive in your collection practices. Call delinquent customers every week if you have to.

▌ Never extend additional credit to anyone who's already late in paying you.

▌ Require a finance charge for any contracts you permit to go unpaid for 60 days or more.

Everyone in business gets stuck with bad debts sometime. So set credit limits that prevent you from winding up with delinquent accounts you can't afford.

Inventory

Don't stock any more materials than you have to. Arrange for partial shipments and billing for large orders whenever you can. If you have security on the site, have materials delivered directly to the job. Materials you have to store cost you extra money for handling, warehousing and insurance. And if you store lots of small items, there's always the problem of not being able to find the things when you need them.

Other Cash Flow Threats

▌ Pilfering: If you've been in construction for a while, you'll know that materials and tools often develop legs and leave the site. Many workers don't think of taking a handful of screws or a drill bit or a piece of lumber as actually stealing. Take steps to make sure this doesn't happen on your site. Lock up small or valuable hardware and parts if necessary. See that no one has access to your warehouse on days you're closed.

▌ Increasing assets: Even though your cash flow looks good at certain stages of the project, this isn't the time to pay off an old loan or invest in new long-term assets. That will only divert cash from your checkbook, where you might need it a few weeks from now.

Last-Ditch Cash Flow Solutions

Remember that cash is the oxygen that feeds the body of your project. Without it, the whole thing will weaken and die. Just as athletes need a good trainer, a business needs experts to guide it toward a winning performance. Think of your office manager and accountant as trainers. Let them monitor cash flow and bring problems to your attention. It's vitally important that you delegate financial activities, especially if you're not strong in those areas, or simply don't have the time.

What if the cash flow pond runs dry? You might have to suspend your draw if you're running a partnership, or cut your own pay if your business is a corporation. Laying off employees is an option, but that's dangerous if it will slow down the job and further delay selling the project and generating income.

When you see a problem, you might have no choice but to cut back your schedule, reduce your labor crews, and slow down the pace. Problems often develop when a company has too much going on at once. Poorly-organized field crews coupled with unreliable subcontractors or slow deliveries can turn a well-ordered project into chaos in short order. It may be time to regroup and reassign your limited number of reliable resources — yourself and your trusted supervisors — to be on the job at all times so no management details are left untended.

Again, don't overlook your lender as a resource to help solve cash flow problems. You both have a stake in the project and should work as partners. Your lender might help by making short-term cash advances, loans or bridge loans to get you through a rough period. If the situation becomes critical, you may need to mortgage your home, or sell other assets.

Another possibility is to request an advance in a phased payment schedule. But beware of this solution. If you start drawing loan proceeds ahead of your completion schedule, you'll run out of capital before the job is finished. Make this a one-time stopgap action taken only in combination with a solid plan for getting back on schedule within a specified short time.

Some of these moves are pretty drastic. That's why it's important that your cash flow projections are accurate to begin with, and that you monitor them closely. If you do that, you'll spot emerging problems and solve them before you have to start skipping meals.

Good project management is all about asking the right questions:

- Are workers performing efficiently?
- Are costs and expenses in line with forecasts?
- Is the project on schedule?
- Are the customers still available and willing to buy?

People who ask the right questions and come up with the best answers are confident about the outcome of their ventures. They've honestly faced the difficult process of verifying their assumptions. They've set goals and created a detailed plan which they followed through to completion. There's a name for such people: *Successful*.

And you can be one of them!

Sample Business Plan

The following pages contain a sample business plan outline. The text demonstrates how the required parts of the plan go together. Your own plan will, of course, be very different, but you can use this sample as a guide to organize and present your plan.

Include your market study in the business plan. Our sample market study outline is in the attachments section of the sample business plan. If your business plan runs to more than 15 pages or so, it's better to bind the market study and its attachments separately. Do the same for financial worksheets and other documents you reference on your forecast and budget, cash flow projection and financial statements.

> Flagged text prompts you about what information to fill in on your own business plan

Anderson Development, Inc

Business Plan.
March 2001
Copy L-1

> **Use your own disclaimer or confidentiality statement**

1

Table of Contents

Introduction

Anderson Development plans to acquire and develop 40 acres of land into a residential community of 65 homes over the next year. Critical to the success of this plan is financing for these activities:

- Land acquisition
- Development of services
- Construction

Our business plan provides that all borrowed funds will be repaid within one year from completion of the project, and assumes this can be done even in a slow real estate market.

We have intentionally used cautious estimates to ensure that our plan is realistic. We expect that actual outcome will exceed forecast sales and profits, and that estimated turnaround time will be shorter than predicted.

A detailed description of your company, including its stage of development

Anderson Development, Inc. was incorporated in 1996. The owners have been active in the local business community for more than 20 years. The company has formerly specialized in single-family housing. During past years we have concentrated on home remodeling and custom home construction or small tracts of 20 or fewer units.

The concepts that drive your company set it apart from others like it and make it unique

Anderson Development maintains relatively low overhead by subcontracting specialized services rather than adding permanently to our own staff. We feel this lets us emphasize high quality over high volume.

Market opportunities that point to success of your development project

Local real estate values have risen steadily in predictable cycles over the past 20 years. Employment in the region remains consistently high, and recent trends reported by the Chamber of Commerce indicate that new employers are finding the area attractive. Their studies promise that new employers will create more than 200 new blue- and white-collar jobs over the next two to three years.

Reference: Market Study, page 19.

Describe your site by location and attributes which make it ideal for your project

The site we've chosen is located on the north side of town, convenient to transportation corridors, employment centers, schools, and commercial outlets. Services, which do not already exist on the property, have been approved for extension into the tract.

We have been assured that the land in question for our development is appropriate for rezone. To the immediate south, two additional tracts have been constructed in recent years. A boulevard connecting to arterial routes into the city already runs to those tracts and can be easily extended to ours.

3

With that in mind, we plan a phased development that will produce 10 to 20 homes per month beginning six months after the project start date, with all units reaching the market by the end of one year. Current market statistics support this.

Reference: Market Study, page 19.

Your competitive advantage

We are well placed among our competitors in the area in terms of capital resources and experience. We've researched their current activities and determined that the current robust economy and housing market will adequately support our planned development as well as those currently under way by other local developers.

Reference: Market Study, page 19.

Your management team's virtues: expertise and accomplishments

Reference: Résumés, publicity, awards, etc.

Milestones or achievements in your company's history

Two prior projects, Anderson Development's first entries into tract development, were each completed ahead of schedule and under budget. Financing on one of these projects was paid off ahead of schedule.

Financial details about how much cash you need, whether you have other investors and how much they're in for, how you'll use the money, and how you'll pay it back

This plan calls for 70 percent financing to purchase the required 40 acres of raw land. The current owner of that land has agreed to participate as a joint venture partner. His share of the development profits will be 30 percent of net. This joint venture is provided to the owner in lieu of a down payment. The landowner has agreed to assumption of a passive role, and will not be active in the management of the business nor in the project itself.

Reference: Joint Venture Partnership Agreement, available on request.

Additional funding will be required to finance necessary rezoning of the property, permits, installation of services, and construction. The entire project will occur in phases, all to be completed within 12 months from the start date. The first phase, including construction of no fewer than 10 homes, will begin immediately upon approval of financing. Subsequent phases will follow at three to four week intervals thereafter.

Reference: Project Schedule, page 7.

Anderson Development will work exclusively on the proposed project for the duration of the 12-month project. Accordingly, all existing overhead will continue, while income will not be generated until approximately four months into the project. This business plan assumes that it will be possible to obtain financing with staged proceeds, and with repayment schedules to begin four months after initial funding.

Reference: Please refer to the Cash Flow Projections, page 12.

4

The ideal financing arrangement will allow Anderson Development the right to prepay the loan based upon sales volume and the likelihood of pre-sold units.

Reference: Marketing Plan, page 19.

Our projections indicate that Anderson Development will be able to repay the entire $2 million loan plus interest and pay our joint venture partner 30 percent of net profits (before calculating our yield), and still generate a net profit to the company of 8 percent, when comparing pre-tax profits to gross sales.

Reference: Pro forma Income Statement, page 6, and Cash Flow Projections, page 12.

Anderson Development, Inc.
Pro forma Income Statement
12 Months ending December 2000

Income, prior contracts	$ 55,000
Income from Sale of Units	9,875,000
Total Sales	$9,930,000
Cost of Goods Sold:	
Materials	$2,338,700
Commissions	593,500
Labor and Subcontracts	2,587,500
Total Cost of Goods Sold	$5,519,700
Gross Profit	$4,410,300
General Expenses:	
Salaries and Wages	$ 168,000
Payroll Taxes	18,300
Rent	15,900
Utilities	2,245
Telephone	1,555
Office	750
Automotive and Truck	4,600
Dues and Subscriptions	330
Operating Supplies	340
Repairs and Maintenance	2,700
Equipment Rental	4,620
Insurance	15,000
Interest	183,200
Legal and Accounting	11,400
Total General Expenses	$ 428,940
Net Profit	$3,981,360

6

Forecast and Budget

The following forecast (of income and costs) and budget (of expenses) is based on several assumptions, including:

1. Existing construction-related income will be received only to the extent of collecting outstanding accounts and completing unfinished work. No new construction contracts will be sought during the coming year other than the project under consideration within this business plan.

2. The financing sought for acquisition, development, and construction will be granted and the repayment schedule described in this budget will be accepted.

3. The market is as strong as we believe and units will sell as scheduled in this business plan.

4. It will be possible to repay the entire $2 million loan plus interest; and to pay our joint venture partner 30 percent of net profits (before calculating our yield), and still generate a net profit to the company of 8 percent, when comparing pre-tax profits to gross sales.

5. The only change to the proposed schedule will be seasonal. The project is scheduled to begin in the fall and take one year, with potential acceleration to the schedule beginning in the spring and lasting through the summer. A delay in beginning the one-year plan will translate to acceleration occurring sooner, which will be a positive change in terms of repayments to the lender.

Each classification reported on the forecast and budget is based on detailed assumption worksheets and documentation, which will be used throughout the project for comparisons between actual income, costs, and expenses. Variances will be identified as to cause, which will allow us to reverse any unfavorable trends.

Reference: Forecast and Budget worksheets, available on request.

Summarize the project schedule: top level phases and activities showing elapsed time or dates

---

7

Anderson Development, Inc.
Forecast and Budget
Residential Development Project: One Year

	Month 1	Month 2	Month 3	YTD Total
Income, prior contracts	$ 35,000	$ 15,000	$ 5,000	$ 55,000
Income from Sale of Units	0	0	430,000	430,000
Total Sales	$ 35,000	$ 15,000	$435,000	$485,000
Cost of Goods Sold:				
Materials	99,500	92,300	90,800	282,600
Commissions	0	0	25,800	25,800
Labor and Subcontracts	207,000	207,000	207,000	621,000
Total Cost of Goods Sold	306,500	299,300	323,600	929,400
Gross Profit	$(271,500)	$(284,300)	$111,400	$(444,400)
General Expenses:				
Salaries and Wages	$ 13,000	$ 13,000	$ 13,000	$ 39,000
Payroll Taxes	1,450	1,450	1,450	4,350
Rent	1,200	1,200	1,200	3,600
Utilities	215	235	270	720
Telephone	85	85	85	255
Office	50	50	50	150
Automotive and Truck	350	350	350	1,050
Dues and Subscriptions	30	0	100	130
Operating Supplies	15	20	20	55
Repairs and Maintenance	200	200	200	600
Equipment Rental	385	385	385	1,155
Insurance	1,250	1,250	1,250	3,750
Interest	16,600	18,300	20,100	55,000
Legal and Accounting	900	900	900	2,700
Total General Expenses	$ 35,730	$ 37,425	$ 39,360	$112,515
Net Profit (Loss)	$(307,230)	$(321,725)	$ 72,040	$(556,915)

8

Anderson Development, Inc.
Forecast and Budget
Residential Development Project: One Year

	Month 4	Month 5	Month 6	YTD Total
Income, prior contracts	$ 0	$ 0	$ 0	$ 55,000
Income from Sale of Units	660,000	745,000	890,000	2,725,000
Total Sales	$ 660,000	$ 745,000	$890,000	$2,780,000
Cost of Goods Sold:				
Materials	174,000	184,000	261,000	901,600
Commissions	39,600	44,700	54,400	164,500
Labor and Subcontracts	214,000	245,000	320,000	1,400,000
Total Cost of Goods Sold	$ 427,600	$ 473,700	$ 635,400	$ 2,466,100
Gross Profit	$ 232,400	$ 271,300	$ 254,600	$ 313,900
General Expenses:				
Salaries and Wages	$ 13,000	$ 13,000	$ 13,000	$ 78,000
Payroll Taxes	1,450	1,450	1,450	8,700
Rent	1,200	1,200	1,200	7,200
Utilities	200	135	120	1,175
Telephone	85	85	85	510
Office	50	50	50	300
Automotive and Truck	350	350	350	2,100
Dues and Subscriptions	0	0	0	130
Operating Supplies	20	25	25	125
Repairs and Maintenance	200	200	200	1,200
Equipment Rental	385	385	385	2,310
Insurance	1,250	1,250	1,250	7,500
Interest	55,000	22,100	24,300	128,100
Legal and Accounting	900	900	900	5,400
Total General Expenses	41,190	43,330	45,715	242,750
Net Profit	191,210	227,970	208,885	71,150

9

Anderson Development, Inc.
Forecast and Budget
Residential Development Project: One Year

	Month 7	Month 8	Month 9	YTD Total
Income, prior contracts	$ 0	$ 0	$ 0	$ 55,000
Income from Sale of Units	950,000	1,100,000	1,300,000	6,075,000
Total Sales	$ 950,000	$1,100,000	$1,300,000	$6,130,000
Cost of Goods Sold:				
Materials	$ 191,000	$ 221,000	$ 261,300	$1,574,900
Commissions	57,000	66,000	78,000	365,500
Labor and Subcontracts	137,500	175,000	225,000	1,937,500
Total Cost of Goods Sold	$ 385,500	$ 462,000	$ 564,300	$ 3,877,900
Gross Profit	$ 564,500	$ 638,000	$ 735,700	$2,252,100
General Expenses:				
Salaries and Wages	$ 15,000	$ 15,000	$ 15,000	$ 123,000
Payroll Taxes	1,600	1,600	1,600	13,500
Rent	1,200	1,500	1,500	11,400
Utilities	250	225	250	1,900
Telephone	115	115	115	855
Office	75	75	75	525
Automotive and Truck	400	400	425	3,325
Dues and Subscriptions	50	0	100	280
Operating Supplies	30	35	35	225
Repairs and Maintenance	250	250	250	1,950
Equipment Rental	385	385	385	3,465
Insurance	1,250	1,250	1,250	11,250
Interest	15,000	13,500	11,700	168,300
Legal and Accounting	1,000	1,000	1,000	8,400
Total General Expenses	$ 36,605	$ 35,335	$ 33,685	$ 348,375
Net Profit	$ 527,895	$ 602,665	$ 702,015	$1,903,725

10

Anderson Development, Inc.
Forecast and Budget
Residential Development Project: One Year

	Month 10	Month 11	Month 12	YTD Total
Income, prior contracts	$ 0	$ 0	$ 0	$ 55,000
Income from Sale of Units	1,500,000	1,300,000	1,000,000	9,875,000
Total Sales	$1,500,000	$1,300,000	$1,000,000	$9,930,000
Cost of Goods Sold:				
Materials	$ 301,500	$ 261,300	$ 201,000	$2,338,700
Commissions	90,000	78,000	60,000	593,500
Labor and Subcontracts	275,000	225,000	150,000	2,587,500
Total Cost of Goods Sold	$ 666,500	$ 564,300	$ 411,000	$5,519,700
Gross Profit	$ 833,500	$ 735,700	$ 589,000	$4,410,300
General Expenses:				
Salaries and Wages	$ 15,000	$ 15,000	$ 15,000	$ 168,000
Payroll Taxes	1,600	1,600	1,600	18,300
Rent	1,500	1,500	1,500	15,900
Utilities	115	115	115	2,245
Telephone	225	225	250	1,555
Office	75	75	75	750
Automotive and Truck	425	425	425	4,600
Dues and Subscriptions	50	0	0	330
Operating Supplies	35	35	45	340
Repairs and Maintenance	250	250	250	2,700
Equipment Rental	385	385	385	4,620
Insurance	1,250	1,250	1,250	15,000
Interest	8,300	5,000	1,600	183,200
Legal and Accounting	1,000	1,000	1,000	11,400
Total General Expenses	$ 30,210	$ 26,860	$ 23,495	$ 428,940
Net Profit	$ 803,290	$ 708,840	$ 565,505	$3,981,360

11

Anderson Development, Inc.
Cash Flow Projections
Residential Development Project: One Year

	Month 1	Month 2	Month 3
Beginning balance	$ 6,079	$ 23,849	$ 27,124
Plus:			
Net profits (losses)	$ (307,230)	$ (321,725)	$ 72,040
Loan proceeds (proposed)	825,000	825,000	450,000
Less:			
Loan principal payments			
Land purchase	(500,000)	(500,000)	(500,000)
30% net paid to partner			
Balance forward	$ 23,849	$ 27,124	$ 49,164

	Month 4	Month 5	Month 6
Balance forward	$ 49,164	$ 240,374	$ 68,334
Plus:			
Net profits (losses)	$ 191,210	$ 227,970	$208,885
Loan proceeds (proposed)			
Less:			
Loan principal payments		(400,000)	
Land purchase			
30% net paid to partner			(21,345)
Balance forward	$ 240,374	$ 68,334	$ 255,884

12

Anderson Development, Inc.
Cash Flow Projections
Residential Development Project: One Year

	Month 7	Month 8	Month 9
Balance forward	$ 255,884	$ 25,410	$ 247,276
Plus:			
Net profits (losses)	$ 527,895	$ 602,665	$ 702,015
Loan proceeds (proposed)			
Less:			
Loan principal payments	(200,000)	(200,000)	(200,000)
Land purchase (400,000)	(400,000)		
30% net paid to partner	(158,369)	(180,799)	(210,605)
	$ 25,410	$ 247,276	$ 138,686
Balance forward			

	Month 10	Month 11	Month 12
Balance forward	$ 138,686	$ 200,989	$ 397,177
Plus:			
Net profits (losses)	$ 803,290	$ 708,840	$ 565,505
Loan proceeds (proposed)			
Less:			
Loan principal payments	(300,000)	(300,000)	(400,000)
Land purchase		(200,000)	
30% net paid to partner	(240,987)	(212,652)	(169,651)
Balance forward	$ 200,989	$ 397,177	$ 393,031

13

Marketing Plan

Describe how you will sell the project

Anderson Development has entered into a contract with County Home, Inc., the largest local real estate brokerage firm. This contract gives County Home, Inc. the exclusive listing of all homes within this development, and is contingent upon approval of financing for this project.

County Home will receive a 6 percent commission on all sales, with a 3 percent bonus for any and all sales made in advance of completion. We anticipate that many of the homes in this development will be pre-sold, which further aids cash flow and loan repayment scheduling.

Such sales, based upon plans only or inspection of models or partially-constructed homes, are not unusual. In fact, in markets such as the one currently seen locally, this is quite common and popular for several reasons.

1. It allows a homeowner certainty as to completion and availability dates, without requiring the payment of mortgage interest in advance of actual date of possession.

2. It enables the home buyer to select inside and outside paint colors and combinations (within a prescribed range of choices), as well as carpet and drapery options.

3. Should a potential buyer wish to modify a plan, Anderson Development is willing and able to customize a specific home to suit a buyer's needs.

14

Financial Statements

> This can be a photocopy of the certification from your CPA or accountant

To Whom It May Concern:

I have prepared the enclosed balance sheet, income statement and statement of cash flows, from the books and records of [*your company name*]. I have performed annual full audits on the company and quarterly full reviews. In my opinion, the books and records reflect an accurate summary of the condition and transactions of the corporation, and conform to generally-accepted auditing standards.

The latest results, as reflected in these statements, were taken directly from the books and records of the company, and are a compilation only. These are not meant to represent a complete or full audit of the books and records.

[Signed by the CPA]

15

Anderson Development Company
Balance Sheet
August 31, 2000

Current Assets:		
Cash	$ 6,079	
Accounts Receivable	55,000	
Inventory	18,500	
Total Current Assets		$ 79,579
Long-term Assets:		
Furniture and Fixtures	$ 10,996	
Equipment and Machinery	118,450	
Small Tools	4,105	
Truck and Automotive	32,643	
Subtotal	$166,194	
Accumulated Depreciation	32,604	
Net Long-term Assets		$133,590
Total Assets		$213,169
Current Liabilities:		
Accounts Payable	$ 5,004	
Taxes Payable	1,600	
Total Current Liabilities	$ 6,604	
Long-term Liabilities	$ 0	
Total Liabilities		$ 6,604
Net Worth		$206,565
Total Liabilities and Net Worth		$213,169

16

Anderson Development, Inc.
Income Statement
For the Eight Months Ending August 31, 2000

Gross Sales		$ 1,100,725
Cost of Goods Sold:		
Beginning Inventory	$ 14,240	
Materials	397,823	
Labor and Subcontractors	266,956	
	$ 679,019	
Less: Ending Inventory	18,500	
Cost of Goods Sold		$ 660,519
Gross Profit		$ 446,206
General Expenses:		
Salaries and Wages	$ 146,000	
Payroll Taxes	17,105	
Rent	14,400	
Utilities	2,110	
Telephone	1,065	
Office	605	
Automotive and Truck	4,062	
Depreciation	7,250	
Dues and Subscriptions	321	
Operating Supplies	209	
Repairs and Maintenance	2,790	
Equipment Rental	4,620	
Insurance	11,315	
Interest	1,794	
Legal and Accounting	12,300	
Total General Expenses		$ 225,946
Net Profit		$ 220,260

17

Anderson Development, Inc.
Statement of Cash Flows
For the Eight Months Ending August 31, 2000

Sources of Funds:

Net profits from operations	$220,260
Plus non-cash expenses:	
Depreciation	7,250
Loan proceeds	12,000
From sale of capital assets	9,662
Total Sources of Funds	$ 249,172

Applications of Funds:

Loan principal payments	$ 12,000
Purchase of capital assets	94,000
Draw for living expenses	100,000
Reduction in Long-term Liabilities	13,506
Total Applications of Funds	$ 219,506

Increase in Funds	$ 29,666

Changes in Working Capital:	Beginning	End	Change
Cash	$ 10,354	$ 6,079	$ (4,275)
Accounts Receivable	42,701	55,000	12,299
Inventory	12,000	18,500	6,500
Accounts Payable	(9,756)	(5,004)	4,752
Current Notes Payable	(12,000)	0	12,000
Taxes Payable	0	(1,610)	(1,610)
Total Changes	$ 43,299	$ 72,965	$ 29,666

18

Attachments

Market Study

> **Provide an introduction which gives an overview of your market study results**

Summary

The market trend for residential demand in this county has followed a strong upward pattern for the past three years. Cycles over the past 30 years show high demand periods of five to eight years separated by two- to three-year flattening-out periods. Past history points to our prediction that a healthy market will exist for our project and will extend for several years after the project is completed.

Based upon studies of housing costs, climate, quality of educational facilities, crime levels, employment, and other economic and social factors, this county is highly rated for quality of life.

Local residential property tax rates are reasonable, and tax revenues are well-managed for the following reasons:

1. Combined city and county government cuts the cost of providing services and eliminates duplication.

2. Consistent, efficient local government controls costs.

3. An ordinance limits tax increases based on a formula tied to population growth.

4. Agreements with neighboring counties let this county share the cost of providing utility services to rural areas.

5. Permits are fast-tracked and efficient, resulting in lower costs passed on to home buyers.

The local market for new housing comes from three primary sources:

1. New families moving to the area, attracted by newly-created jobs. Homeowners attracted from outside the area transfer equity from other properties and bring cash into the local economy.

2. Current residents trading up to newer or larger homes. This consistent and reliable market has developed and expanded over several decades.

   Reference: Local Chamber of Commerce study dated June 2000

3. First-time home buyers. The average age of first-time buyers in this county is 26, compared with the state average of 31, and their annual income exceeds that of the state average for their age group by $4,700.

   Reference: Governor's Report to the Legislature, 2000, County breakdown of statistics, pp. 68-73

> **Attach the market study summaries you prepared as described in Chapters 2 and 6**

19

Our Competition

Anderson Development is not the only developer in this community, nor are we the largest or best capitalized. However, we believe that we can provide the best quality within our defined market range.

We view ourselves as competitors in a mid-range of companies, which can be defined roughly as generating between $1 million and $20 million in sales per year. Companies below that range would not be competitors for the development we propose because of their general lack of experience, capital and personnel resources. On the other hand, much larger construction firms are likely to focus on projects which take better advantage of their high level of capitalization, large investment in equipment and facilities, and specialized personnel.

Within our defined range, Anderson Development has four direct competitors in the community. Two of those are currently engaged in commercial projects. The other two are not expected to compete significantly for the market share we've identified for our development since the market study indicates there are more than enough buyers out there now for all of us.

As the area continues to expand in terms of job base, population, and infrastructure, we may expect that additional competitors will come into the picture; and that some of the present competitors will expand upward. We believe we can maintain a lead position within this mid-range. We do not wish to expand beyond the broad range described here, but we do expect to dominate that range within the community, and to continue to strive for a lead role in the residential development industry.

One potential strategy for the future may be to enter joint ventures with one or more of our competitors; or to merge two companies into one. We're not considering this for our present project due to our excellent credit position and the willingness of the landowner to participate as a joint venture partner.

Trends for Our Development Class

Single-family housing regularly beats inflation and grows in value both nationally and locally. The idea of home ownership is highly valued among Americans, and this creates a steadily-increasing demand for new housing units.

Residential Trends

Illustrate statistical information using charts or graphs

Housing construction has enjoyed healthy growth for the past 20 years, with relatively steady demand throughout that period. Slowdowns have occurred in conjunction with the employment cycle. But employment has also risen steadily over the past two decades, with no less than a 3 percent increase every year, and some years seeing as much as 7 percent growth.

Owner-occupied housing represents 97 percent of total housing units in the county. This exceeds national averages. (The percentage of owner-occupied units is considered an indicator of a community's housing values. The higher the percentage, the better, in terms of long-term appreciation and neighborhood value.)

Reference: Chamber of Commerce Survey

New unit development has increased an average of 4 percent every year. The "spread" (percentage difference between asked prices and sales prices of homes) has never exceeded 5 percent during the past 20 years, with most years showing a spread of 2 to 3 percent. Average time homes remain on the market is under 30 days.

20

Reference: County Board of Real Estate; Multiple Listing Service, "Statistics," December 2000

Our current development plan calls for construction of homes that will sell in the mid-range of $115,000 to $130,000. This is the range that's most attractive to new-home buyers in the community, and thus represents the price range that remains on the market for the least amount of time.

Reference: County Board of Real Estate; Multiple Listing Service, "Statistics" (various months)

Local Land Prices

Use real numbers when you furnish information like this

Our community has seen a gradual and steady growth in land values over many years. Cyclical changes have tended to be mild and short-term. On average, prices of raw land (undeveloped and not served by roads, utilities, and public services) have grown between 1 and 2 percent per year. However, as raw land has been improved or developed, its value increased significantly.

An abundance of raw land is available at low prices, but most of those parcels are 10 acres or less. These were impractical for our development plan because we need to spread the costs of public services among many buyers to make them affordable.

Raw land in plots of adequate size is relatively scarce in this community. Of the potential sites that exist, few are currently on the market, especially in truly raw condition. Several partially-serviced sites are for sale, most already zoned for residential use. For our purposes, the cost of these parcels is prohibitive for our modestly-priced homes.

Our solution was to locate our joint venture partner who is willing to sell part of his undeveloped 80 acres. We have agreed to exercise a currently-held option to buy 40 acres contingent upon financing approval. We anticipate financing 70 percent of the purchase price, with the current owner carrying the remainder as a joint venture share. That entitles the owner to 30 percent of our net profits from the development.

We have anticipated the costs associated with acquiring the necessary rezoning, complying with environmental requirements, and getting permits. These costs, added to the cost of the land, are still reasonable in terms of our providing affordable, well-constructed houses.

Reference: Land Market Study documents

Local Demographics and Economy

Recent trends show that a healthy and continuing increase in the job base and steadily growing value of real estate have changed the county from a depressed rural area 20 years ago, to one of the most economically robust areas in the state. We believe this trend will continue, and that the development of quality but affordable homes is an essential part of the community's growth.

Reference: State Department of Economic Development report, October 2000

While researching the recent trends in the job market, we considered only full-time employment statistics, believing that our local, relatively-large college-aged population with part-time employment (especially in retail) distort the trend in family wages. The average full-time salary exceeds the state average by 14 percent. The average local full-time wage level has grown over the past 20 years — most notably in the last five years — by more than 20 percent, as new employers have moved into the area.

21

Reference: U.S. Census Bureau; Office of Economic Development, Annual Report, Appendix C

We believe these trends will continue. Employment will continue to rise in the next five to ten years. We know of no fewer than 15 corporations looking for relocation sites in our county now, with plans to locate light manufacturing and warehousing facilities here within the next two to three years.

Reference: Chamber of Commerce Business Development Division, Annual Report

Several hundred new jobs will be created in this county if these plans come to pass. In addition, Job Outlook Magazine (February 2000) reports that every new job creates 1.6 additional jobs, each of which will add to the community's employment base.

While statewide population growth is estimated to occur over the next 20 years at 1.5 percent overall, our county's growth is estimated at 4 percent.

Reference: Office of Economic Development, Annual Report, p. 55

Facilities for three new companies are already under construction. Those businesses will create more than 300 new jobs within the coming year. All those employees will need housing. At this time, an estimated 8 percent of the local workforce commutes here from outside the county, and apartment vacancy rates are near zero.

Reference: Office of Economic Development, quarterly market survey, p. 10; Multiple Listing Service, "Apartment Survey," Spring, 2000

Politics and the Local Market

The political "market" is extremely important and cannot be ignored by potential developers.

The county government is currently characterized by a pro-growth majority. In recent years, the county executive and council have worked with economic and business interests to attract new employers to the area, to create a healthy job climate, to stabilize the housing market and reduce housing costs, and to lower the cost of local government.

We believe there is no reason to expect this to change in the near future. Our project is estimated to take one year from the date of approval of financing. The next election is two years away. The political climate tends to affect development only during the application phases, which include:

- Initial review and approval (or rejection)
- Environmental review
- Permitting

These steps will be completed within two to four months from approval of financing. After that, an approved project will be able to proceed on schedule.

As evidence of the health of our local political situation, the council has entered into a cooperative agreement with the Office of Economic Development, the purpose of which is to attract new employers to the area. This program includes a coordinated effort between legislative and executive branches of county government, development of promotional literature about our county, and fast-track permit approval procedures. The county also recently enacted an ordinance giving new employers reductions in first-year property taxes based on new job creation.

Another indicator of political health was a recent program initiated by the county council to actively solicit business relocation to our county. Initial response shows that a lot of statewide interest is being generated, notably from companies currently located in the larger urban areas. They are attracted to this

22

area by relatively cheap undeveloped land, a spirit of cooperation at City Hall, low taxes, and a pro-growth attitude on the part of elected officials, planning staff, and the citizens of this county.

Anderson Development has participated in several joint meetings of the planning commission and county council as a member of a business advisory group to offer recommendations to the planning department for speeding up processes and improving work, while reducing unnecessary delay. We find this activity rewarding because local government is listening and taking advice from the business community.

A separate long-range planning department is responsible for growth projections, growth management programming, and coordination of city and county issues. That department has worked with Anderson Development in designing a proposed street plan for the project, planning utilities, and beginning the process of annexation.

We considered the sensitivity of our proposal to local opposition in the planning stages, not only in terms of how impacts must be mitigated, but also for other considerations such as impacts on traffic patterns and the environment.

Risk Management

Anderson Development is aware of the risks involved in this project, and this business plan is designed to address those risks. We have identified the major risks and demonstrated how we will address each one.

Summarize your responses under these headings

Interest Rate Risk

We address this risk in two ways.

1. The financing plan is very short-term, so lenders are not being asked to carry an outstanding note for many years. The note will be repaid within one year, as the property is developed and sold.

2. We are willing to negotiate conditions with a lender for variable rates based on the lender's own cost of borrowing. If the federal funds rate changes during the period the loan is outstanding, we are willing to have the corresponding increase passed on to us by contract. However, we also ask that if the federal funds rate is reduced, that our rate be lowered in the same manner.

Market Risk

We are confident that the market risk is minimal based on the information provided above in the sections on trends and demographics. We know we need buyers for the homes we plan to build. If buyers were scarce, our asked price would be forced downward. But our research shows there is an abundance of buyers in the market for homes in our price range who will support our asked price and our final profit.

23

Competition Risk

In our analysis of our local competition, there was nothing to indicate that their activities will threaten our success in this project at this time. In fact, because Anderson Development maintains a cordial relationship with other builders in the area, it's entirely possible that our defined competitors will join us on this project as subcontractors.

A second risk could be that a better-financed company, either local or from outside the area, would be able to complete a project more quickly and for less cost, translating to more competitive pricing of homes and a better market share. Again, the current seller's market combined with our presence and reputation in the area work to minimize this risk.

Personal Risk

To eliminate the risk of the illness, injury to or death of a key management person, delaying the project, Anderson Development has arranged for accident, disability and life insurance for all of its key employees. We further understand that the lender may require that we assign benefits and designate the lender as beneficiary under key personnel policies, for the period of time that loans remain outstanding.

Business Reversal Risk

A lender will certainly be aware of the great risk involved in business reversal — meaning the failure of the organization, due to poor planning, unforeseen outside influences, or bad timing economically.

Such risks cannot be eliminated entirely; they can only be reduced through thorough and complete planning. We believe that our business plan documents the fact that our assumptions are solid, and that we have a better-than-average chance of succeeding in this plan.

Additionally, Anderson Development has been active in construction and development activities in this community for more than four years, and its owners have been involved in the business for more than two decades. We are firmly-established members of the community, not new arrivals or untested new business owners. Business reversal can happen to any company at any time, but the facts of this matter mitigate this risk.

Inexperience Risk

An inexperienced business owner invariably suffers when unexpected problems arise. Another way of expressing "inexperience risk" would be to call it "surprise risk." The benefit of experience is that the owners come to expect the unexpected, to plan for it, and to remain calm while solving new problems.

Anderson Development has years of experience in many construction and development projects, primarily in the residential sector. However, the proposed project is admittedly our most ambitious proposal to date. The level of financing, likewise, is substantial and represents a significant expansion above prior levels of activity by the company.

We believe that our experience in past projects, similar but smaller in size, prepares us to tackle this project. The types of problems that will arise will be identical to those previously encountered, and not beyond Anderson's ability to solve.

Profit and Loss Risk

Every expansion and every business enterprise has to be concerned with the potential problem of losing money. We always believe we will have a profit from all of the activities we undertake. Of course, that doesn't always happen.

Business owners have to approach large projects — like the proposed one — from the point of view that they consider the opportunity, the risks, and the likely outcome, and make reasonable efforts to correctly estimate the future. We believe that by preparing a business plan and market study, we can prove our assumptions are realistic. We have determined:

- We have a market for this much housing in this price range.

- Our schedule is realistic.

- The plan has built-in leeway for unexpected problems.

- The numbers "work."

These facts lead us to the conclusion that while the risk of losing money is present in all ventures, we believe that the current demand, our own experience in building houses, the local mood in support of this plan, and our caution in preparing our plan, all decrease the risk of financial loss.

Cash Flow Risk

Anderson Development discovered many years ago that cash flow must be controlled, and problems have to be anticipated far in advance to avoid the risk of losing control over working capital. We have put a procedure in place for review of cash flow as part of our forecast and budget review. The half day per month that we spend studying the prior month's variances of forecasts, budgets, and projections is among the most valuable of our administrative operations. We intend to institute a twice-monthly review process during the proposed project, to ensure that our cash flow remains tightly controlled. We also contend that our proposed cash flow projection includes many conservative assumptions, and that we will exceed our own estimates on the positive side.

Is the Timing Right?

Local indicators are the only ones that count when it comes to timing the market. Local supply and demand cycles for single-family housing, for financing, and for the job market, all affect the timing of development.

One of the risks that lender and developer share is the risk that timing might be wrong. The current economic cycle can change suddenly and without warning, although a careful study of the market usually yields a dependable estimate of near-term future changes. In our community, the local factors have shown steady and reliable indicators over many years, and the future promises more of the same. Construction and development grow from many dependable factors, as well as reliance on future trends. Known factors today include very low unemployment, a recent history of good job growth and housing prices, few available houses on the market, and several employers currently constructing light manufacturing facilities in the south end of town. These will create additional housing demand in coming years.

We believe that we are correct in our analysis of today's local market as being strong today and remaining strong well beyond the next year.

We believe the timing is right to begin construction of this project as soon as possible.

Goals and Assumptions Worksheets

Goal # 1

Define a realistic, workable plan to acquire 40 acres north of town, for the purpose of developing those acres for residential use: Completion: one month.

Assumptions:

1. The land is for sale at a price acceptable to Anderson Development, Inc. (already established)

2. The seller will give Anderson Development an option. (already completed)

3. A plan based upon the initial ideas for development of the 40 acres in question will be profitable.

4. It will be possible to obtain a rezone to residential for the land (to be achieved before exercising the option).

Steps	Due date	Completed
1. Investigate the current market to determine whether this idea is realistic	3/15	
2. Approach owner and attempt to obtain an option to buy	3/25	
3. Write a preliminary market study and business plan	3/31	3/31

26

Goal # 2

Complete a detailed market study and business plan demonstrating how the associated risks of the project will be managed and minimized. Completion: three months.

Assumptions

1. A business plan will support the proposed development plan.

2. The market study will support Anderson Development's belief that a strong market exists for new residential development in this county.

3. The risks associated with this project are not beyond the abilities of Anderson Development.

4. A lender will review the business plan and market study and come to the same conclusion: that financing the proposed development is an acceptable risk.

Steps	Due date	Completed
1. Search local sources for market information	3/20	
2. Compile recent trend summary to identify market direction	4/30	
3. Identify likely direction of residential housing market; housing prices; job markets; and other economic factors	5/20	
4. List risks for Anderson Development as well as for potential lending sources; identify how those risks are to be managed over the next year. Write the study and plan.	5/31	5/31

27

Goal # 3

Get approval for rezone of the land. Completion: six months.

Assumptions

1. The county is motivated to develop more residential land, and will recommend and support the rezone request.

2. No serious local opposition to the proposed rezone will present itself.

3. Upon approval of the rezone, it will be possible to exercise the option on the land and to acquire ownership.

4. Financing will be made available for the purchase of the land, at 70 percent of the purchase price.

Steps	Due date	Completed
1. File application for rezone hearing with Planning Department	3/10	
2. Schedule public hearing	3/12	
3. Prepare testimony for hearing, including expert testimony and submission of reports and findings	5/15	
4. Assuming approval from Planning Department: schedule public hearing before County Council	6/1	
5. Submit materials and records for consideration by full Council	8/16	

28

Goal # 4

Get financing for acquisition, development, and construction. Completion: eight months.
Assumptions

1. Financing will be approved for all three phases of this project, based upon this business plan and market study.
2. Financing will be provided on terms acceptable to Anderson Development, Inc.
3. The long-standing experience and background of the owners of Anderson Development, Inc., their excellent credit, and the value of this proposal, will ensure a lender that risks are worth taking.

Steps	Due date	Completed
1. Deliver business plan and market study to lender upon approval by Planning Department	6/10	
2. Meet with lender to discuss specifics of loan segments: acquisition, development, and construction	7/1	
3. Meet with lender upon approval of rezone by County Council	8/1	
4. Meet further conditions for approval of financing	8/15	
5. Target date for loan approval	8/31	

29

Goal # 5

Complete building and sale of units within one year from start of construction.

Assumptions

1. No appeals are filed and Goals 1 through 4 can be completed within six months.
2. Planning Department will provide fast-track permit approval.
3. Construction will occur in two-month phases, with all units completed and sold on schedule.
4. Arranged financing will provide for deferred payments — no repayment for the first four months of the construction phase.

Steps	Target	Completed
1. Exercise option and purchase land in coordination with lender	9/1	
2. Apply for initial permits and contact county public works to schedule installation of utilities and services	9/1	
3. Target date for permit approvals	10/15	
4. Begin construction	11/1	
5. Tentative first-phase completion	1/15	
6. Develop firm schedule for balance of project	1/15	

30

This section contains useful blank copies of the forms and checklists used throughout the book. The author and publisher give you permission to copy and use them in your own business. If they're not exactly what you need, use them as starting points for custom-designed forms and checklists. Just copy them onto your computer from the disk inside the back cover of this book, then add your own letterhead and make any changes. You can then fill out the forms on your computer and print them. Detailed instructions on how to use the disk are on page 223. If you don't use a computer, just photocopy the forms right out of the book and fill them out by hand.

Use forms to enter your data whenever practical. This makes everything uniform, thus easier to retrieve and understand later. A scrap of paper or a notepad are often closer at hand, but they are easily lost, misplaced or thrown away. Chances are, you might not even remember what you meant at the time you jotted down a note to yourself. A form helps ensure that you enter all the data that you're going to need in a standardized manner, not just what you happen to make note of at the time. Forms help you stay organized; you'll have the information you need where and when you need it. And when it comes time to meet with a potential lender, a neatly-filled out set of printed forms is a comfort to any banker or financial backer.

Checklists serve not only to help you keep track of what has been done and what is yet to do, but as "shopping lists" to make sure you don't forget any of the dozens of steps involved in every part of the land development and financing process.

Directory of Forms & Checklists	
Form	Filename
Available Land Analysis	LANDANYS
Market Study Checklist	MSLIST
Parcel Evaluation Checklist	PELIST
Feasibility Analysis	FEASANYS
General Checklist for Lender Interview	LENDLIST
Budget vs. Actual Costs	BUDVSACT
Pro forma Income Statement	PROFORMA
Forecast & Budget	FORECAST
Cash Flow Projections	CASHFLW1
Balance Sheet	BALANCE
Income Statement	INCOME
Statement of Cash Flows	CASHFLW2
Goals & Assumptions Worksheet	GOALS

Available Land Analysis

Total suitable available acres: _____   Number of plots: _____

Site location	Size (acres)	Zoning	Current use	Owner	Cost per acre

Available Land Analysis

Site	1	2	3	4	5	6	7	8	9	10
Location										
Exempt										
Building acres										
Services present										
Water										
Gas										
Electricity										
Telephone										
Cable										
Amenities available										
School										
Hospital										
Fire										
Police										
Trash handling										
Street maintenance										
Public area maintenance										

Market Study Checklist

Your competition

- ☐ Who are your competitors?
- ☐ Are they more or less experienced than you?
- ☐ Are your competitors better or worse off financially than you?
- ☐ What is their annual sales volume?
- ☐ How many people do they employ?
- ☐ What are their specialties?

Trends for your development class

- ☐ How many homes like yours are already for sale?
- ☐ How long do they stay on the market?
- ☐ Who's buying them?
- ☐ How much are buyers paying for them?
- ☐ Are buyers paying close to the asking price?
- ☐ Which age segment of the population are you targeting?
- ☐ How many of those people are there?

Local demographics and economy

- ☐ Are population centers shifting in your area?
- ☐ How many people are moving to or away from your community?
- ☐ What's the breakdown of income levels among local residents?
- ☐ How many and what kinds of jobs are available?
- ☐ How does the population break down by age?
- ☐ Which age brackets are significantly growing or decreasing?
- ☐ How do assessed values for land and improvements compare to those nearby?
- ☐ Analyze crime rates by location.
- ☐ What's the current status of industrial and commercial development?

Politics and your market

- ☐ Will environmentalists resist your plan?
- ☐ What's the ratio between pro-growth and no-growth backers in city/county government?
- ☐ Are planners cooperative with developers?
- ☐ Is there an active movement to attract new business to the area?

Risk management

- ☐ Are there enough potential buyers earning enough to buy your houses?
- ☐ Are interest rates rising, dropping, or remaining stable?
- ☐ Are there signs pointing to an upcoming economic decline?

Parcel Evaluation Checklist

Land characteristics

Define in terms of grading and excavation, foundation requirements.

- ❑ Soil type: Is it sandy, rocky, full of clay?
- ❑ Vegetation: Are there trees you can incorporate as a noise or sight buffer, or as an open space corridor for common use? Or will you clear everything to provide landscaping?
- ❑ Water table, percolation rate: Will these affect foundations and drainage?
- ❑ Flood plane: Near enough to provide a hazard?
- ❑ Elevations: Is the property level? Hilly? Marked by canyons? Are there rock formations that will hamper grading?
- ❑ Earthquake faults: How close and how risky?
- ❑ Water: Lakes, lagoons, rivers, streams or ponds?
- ❑ Other _____

Services

Check those already in place. If not, how much will it cost to provide them, if required?

- ❑ Water _____
- ❑ Gas _____
- ❑ Electricity _____
- ❑ Telephone _____
- ❑ Cable _____
- ❑ Sewers, storm drains _____
- ❑ Trash disposal _____
- ❑ Other _____

Improvements

- ❑ How much will it cost to install services and improvements?
- ❑ What will I have to build?
- ❑ What will I be assessed for?
- ❑ Power lines or transmission towers: Where are they? Will they interfere with my plans?
- ❑ Roads: Location? Are they adequate to handle increased traffic generated by my project?
- ❑ Traffic loads on major streets and highways?
- ❑ Existing buildings: Will I need to demolish them?
- ❑ Transportation infrastructure: Proximity of railroad lines, ports, freeways?
- ❑ Other _____

Amenities

Which of the following are conveniently located or accessible?

- ❑ Grade school
- ❑ Middle school
- ❑ High school
- ❑ Fire protection
- ❑ Law enforcement

Zoning issues

- ❑ Is the property already annexed to the local zoning jurisdiction?
- ❑ If not, is assurance forthcoming that it will be?
- ❑ How is the parcel zoned now?
- ❑ How has the parcel been used In the past?
- ❑ How are nearby or adjacent plots zoned?
- ❑ Are nearby zonings compatible?
- ❑ Local regulatory climate and prospects for rezone?
- ❑ Other _____

Location

- ❑ Is this parcel clearly in the path of progress?
- ❑ Relationship of site to nearby and adjacent properties
- ❑ Access to existing services and amenities
- ❑ Distance to shopping, entertainment, recreation
- ❑ Distance from "undesirable" uses: Trash processing, heavy industrial, etc.
- ❑ Access to transportation links: Freeways, commuter rail, shipping hubs
- ❑ Special benefits of this location for my project

Price

- ❑ Raw land: Will the added cost of improvements exceed our budgeted land cost per building unit?
- ❑ Improved land: Is the increased cost adequately offset by existing improvements?

Environmental conditions

- ❑ Protected wetlands
- ❑ Host to endangered habitat
- ❑ Nearby hazards, natural and man-made
- ❑ Noise levels (existing and resulting from improvements)
- ❑ Percentage of useable land (not restricted by mitigation)
- ❑ Other _____

Feasibility Analysis

Location: _____ **Date:** _____

Street Address: _____

City: _____

Land Costs

Land purchase price _____

Land closing costs _____

Off-site improvement _____

Demolition & clearing _____

On-site improvement _____

Total land costs _____

Development Costs

Survey & topo maps _____

Percolation test _____

Architectural & design services _____

Engineering fees _____

Soil testing _____

Environment testing _____

Plan copies & reprints _____

Market & feasibility studies _____

Appraisal fees _____

Insurance _____

Property taxes _____

Legal & accounting _____

Building permits & fees _____

Utility fees _____

Administration overhead _____

Interest reserve _____

Total development costs _____

Financing Costs

Interest on land _____

Land development _____

Construction loan fees _____

Construction loan closing costs _____

Construction loan interest _____

Total financing costs _____

Construction Costs

Total construction cost _____

Total land cost _____

Total development cost _____

Total finance cost _____

Total construction cost _____

Subtotal project costs _____

Marketing & Closing Costs

Sales commissions _____

Advertising _____

Closing costs _____

Other costs paid by seller _____

Total marketing & closing costs _____

Total Project Cost Summary

Land cost _____

Development cost _____

Financing cost _____

Construction cost _____

Marketing & closing costs _____

Total project costs _____

Analysis Summary

Estimated sales price _____

Total project cost (subtotal) _____

Net profit _____

General Checklist for Lender Interview

Planning checklist

- ❑ Use past information and experience.
- ❑ Develop methods for documenting past activity.
- ❑ Document predictions with past activity in mind.
- ❑ Design your plan as a working document — be prepared to amend it frequently.
- ❑ Use the business plan to monitor and control income, costs and expenses.
- ❑ Use the plan to convince lenders that:
    - A. You are a worthwhile risk.
    - B. You have thought through the problems.
    - C. You are aware of what a lender needs to see.
    - D. You know how to use numbers to make your case.
    - E. You are well-organized.
- ❑ Make sure the plan shows — specifically — what you intend to achieve.
- ❑ Make sure your plan is tied together with goals.
- ❑ Follow your plan and use it as a control document.
- ❑ Revise the plan regularly.

Lender presentation checklist

- ❑ Make sure your plan works — the lender will want to know this.
- ❑ Describe your project clearly, simply, honestly.
- ❑ Include a discussion of the risks, not just potential profits. (Fill out the risk analysis worksheet to prepare for this discussion.)
- ❑ Map out your profit plan.
- ❑ Prepare cash flow summaries to show that you can afford repayments.
- ❑ Demonstrate your management skill in the presentation.
- ❑ Anticipate the lender's questions and answer them in your proposal.
- ❑ Show a track record of using your plan to ensure success.

Market checklist

- ❑ Identify the specific demand and need for your project.
- ❑ Document your claims with marketing statistics.
- ❑ Demonstrate how recent past trends add to your arguments.
- ❑ Talk about the potential resistance to your ideas and how you will deal with it.
- ❑ Tie together your marketing assumptions with dollars and sense:
    - A. What will it cost per unit of construction?
    - B. What is the likely sales price per unit?
    - C. Identify the timing differences between construction and sale.
    - D. Show how you have allowed for delay in the project.
    - E. Identify likely problems and your contingency plan.

- ❑ Who is your target buyer? How will you reach that individual?
- ❑ What demographic information supports your project?
- ❑ What are the current market statistics and competition?
- ❑ Where does your project fit in the local scheme of things?
- ❑ What local benefits will be derived from your project?
  - A. New employment.
  - B. Community benefits.
  - C. Environmental protection.
  - D. Dedication of property as part of your project.
  - E. New housing, workspace, or commercial benefits.

Project site checklist

- ❑ Show how and why the particular site was selected.
- ❑ What benefits does your site offer over others?
  - A. Strategic location.
  - B. Proximity to other services and facilities.
  - C. Appropriate zoning.
  - D. Community plan coordination with your project.
  - E. Plans for development of roads and utilities to your site.
- ❑ What physical features make your site attractive for the project?
- ❑ What physical features are problematical, and how will you mitigate?
- ❑ What impacts of development might be seen by other property owners?
- ❑ How do you plan to mitigate those impacts?
- ❑ Have you budgeted for environmental review and process?
- ❑ Have you budgeted well enough for the cost of environmental mitigation?
- ❑ What extra costs will be involved to prepare the land before actual project construction will be possible (environmental buffers, grading, paving, utilities, etc.)?

Goals checklist

- ❑ Have you listed a series of goals?
- ❑ Are those goals specific and realistic and are they project-related?
- ❑ Do your goals have deadlines?
- ❑ Do goals address essentials such as:
  - A. Financing
  - B. Facilities and equipment
  - C. Personnel
  - D. Subcontractors and suppliers
- ❑ Are goals based on specific assumptions?
- ❑ What is the documented basis for your assumptions?
- ❑ Can you demonstrate that goals can be reached based on information at hand?
- ❑ Do goals and assumptions address risk and propose contingency plans?

Forecast and budget checklist

- ❑ Are all of the numbers in the forecast and budget documented?
- ❑ Do your columns add up?
- ❑ Are your forecasts realistic and based on logical assumptions?
- ❑ Will your forecast and budget support your cash flow requirements?
- ❑ Is the forecast and budget easy to understand?
- ❑ Is the presentation cross-referenced and neat?
- ❑ Is the summary supported with all the necessary detail?
- ❑ Are you prepared to answer any financial question a lender might ask?
- ❑ If you're not comfortable talking about the numbers, are you prepared to visit your lender with your accountant?

Cash flow projection checklist

- ❑ Have you mapped out your cash flow requirements through the project period?
- ❑ Have you demonstrated a realistic use of cash?
- ❑ Does your plan include repayment of borrowed money, with interest?
- ❑ Are there shortfall periods?
- ❑ How will you deal with shortfalls? Does your plan include contingency plans?
- ❑ Have you mapped out the in-and-out and the timing of cash flow?
- ❑ Is the presentation format adequate to demonstrate your planning?

Budget vs. Actual Costs

Description	Actual	Budget	Monthly Difference	YTD Difference
Budget line item)				

BUDVSACT

[Your Company Name]
Pro forma Income Statement
12 Months ending [Date]

Income, prior contracts

Income from Sale of Units _____

Total Sales _____

Cost of Goods Sold:

    Materials _____

    Commissions _____

    Labor and Subcontracts _____

Total Cost of Goods Sold _____

Gross Profit _____

General Expenses:

    Salaries and Wages _____

    Payroll Taxes _____

    Rent _____

    Utilities _____

    Telephone _____

    Office _____

    Automotive and Truck _____

    Dues and Subscriptions _____

    Operating Supplies _____

    Repairs and Maintenance _____

    Equipment Rental _____

    Insurance _____

    Interest _____

    Legal and Accounting _____

Total General Expenses _____

Net Profit _____

[Your Company Name]
Forecast and Budget
[Name] Development Project: One Year

	Month 1	Month 2	Month 3	YTD Total
Income, prior contracts	_____	_____	_____	_____
Income from Sale of Units	_____	_____	_____	_____
Total Sales	_____	_____	_____	_____
Cost of Goods Sold:				
Materials	_____	_____	_____	_____
Commissions	_____	_____	_____	_____
Labor and Subcontracts	_____	_____	_____	_____
Total Cost of Goods Sold	_____	_____	_____	_____
Gross Profit	_____	_____	_____	_____
General Expenses:				
Salaries and Wages	_____	_____	_____	_____
Payroll Taxes	_____	_____	_____	_____
Rent	_____	_____	_____	_____
Utilities	_____	_____	_____	_____
Telephone	_____	_____	_____	_____
Office	_____	_____	_____	_____
Automotive and Truck	_____	_____	_____	_____
Dues and Subscriptions	_____	_____	_____	_____
Operating Supplies	_____	_____	_____	_____
Repairs and Maintenance	_____	_____	_____	_____
Equipment Rental	_____	_____	_____	_____
Insurance	_____	_____	_____	_____
Interest	_____	_____	_____	_____
Legal and Accounting	_____	_____	_____	_____
Total General Expenses	_____	_____	_____	_____
Net Profit (Loss)	_____	_____	_____	_____

[Your Company Name]
Forecast and Budget
[Name] Development Project: One Year

	Month 4	Month 5	Month 6	YTD Total
Income, prior contracts				
Income from Sale of Units				
Total Sales				
Cost of Goods Sold:				
Materials				
Commissions				
Labor and Subcontracts				
Total Cost of Goods Sold				
Gross Profit				
General Expenses:				
Salaries and Wages				
Payroll Taxes				
Rent				
Utilities				
Telephone				
Office				
Automotive and Truck				
Dues and Subscriptions				
Operating Supplies				
Repairs and Maintenance				
Equipment Rental				
Insurance				
Interest				
Legal and Accounting				
Total General Expenses				
Net Profit				

[Your Company Name]
Forecast and Budget
[Name] Development Project: One Year

	Month 7	Month 8	Month 9	YTD Total
Income, prior contracts				
Income from Sale of Units				
Total Sales				
Cost of Goods Sold:				
Materials				
Commissions				
Labor and Subcontracts				
Total Cost of Goods Sold				
Gross Profit				
General Expenses:				
Salaries and Wages				
Payroll Taxes				
Rent				
Utilities				
Telephone				
Office				
Automotive and Truck				
Dues and Subscriptions				
Operating Supplies				
Repairs and Maintenance				
Equipment Rental				
Insurance				
Interest				
Legal and Accounting				
Total General Expenses				
Net Profit				

[Your Company Name]
Forecast and Budget
[Name] Development Project: One Year

	Month 10	Month 11	Month 12	YTD Total
Income, prior contracts				
Income from Sale of Units				
Total Sales				
Cost of Goods Sold:				
Materials				
Commissions				
Labor and Subcontracts				
Total Cost of Goods Sold				
Gross Profit				
General Expenses:				
Salaries and Wages				
Payroll Taxes				
Rent				
Utilities				
Telephone				
Office				
Automotive and Truck				
Dues and Subscriptions				
Operating Supplies				
Repairs and Maintenance				
Equipment Rental				
Insurance				
Interest				
Legal and Accounting				
Total General Expenses				
Net Profit				

[Your Company Name]
Cash Flow Projections
[Project Name] Development Project: One Year

	Month 1	**Month 2**	**Month 3**
Beginning balance	_____	_____	_____
Plus:			
net profits (losses)	_____	_____	_____
loan proceeds (proposed)	_____	_____	_____
Less:			
loan principal payments	_____	_____	_____
land purchase	_____	_____	_____
30% net paid to partner	_____	_____	_____
Balance forward	_____	_____	_____

	Month 4	**Month 5**	**Month 6**
Balance forward	_____	_____	_____
Plus:			
net profits (losses)	_____	_____	_____
loan proceeds (proposed)	_____	_____	_____
Less:			
loan principal payments	_____	_____	_____
land purchase	_____	_____	_____
30% net paid to partner	_____	_____	_____
Balance forward	_____	_____	_____

[Your Company Name]
Cash Flow Projections
[Project Name] Development Project: One Year

	Month 7	**Month 8**	**Month 9**
Balance forward	_____	_____	_____
Plus:			
net profits (losses)	_____	_____	_____
loan proceeds (proposed)	_____	_____	_____
Less:			
loan principal payments	_____	_____	_____
land purchase (400,000)	_____	_____	_____
30% net paid to partner	_____	_____	_____
Balance forward	_____	_____	_____

	Month 10	**Month 11**	**Month 12**
Balance forward	_____	_____	_____
Plus:			
net profits (losses)	_____	_____	_____
loan proceeds (proposed)	_____	_____	_____
Less:			
loan principal payments	_____	_____	_____
land purchase	_____	_____	_____
30% net paid to partner	_____	_____	_____
Balance forward	_____	_____	_____

[Your Company Name]
Balance Sheet
[Date]

Current Assets:

    Cash   _____

    Accounts Receivable   _____

    Inventory   _____

    Total Current Assets   _____

Long-term Assets:

    Furniture and Fixtures   _____

    Equipment and Machinery   _____

    Small Tools   _____

    Truck and Automotive   _____

        Subtotal   _____

        Accumulated Depreciation   _____

    Net Long-term Assets   _____

Total Assets   _____

Current Liabilities:

    Accounts Payable   _____

    Taxes Payable   _____

    Total Current Liabilities   _____

Long-term Liabilities   _____

Total Liabilities   _____

Net Worth   _____

Total Liabilities and Net Worth   _____

[Your Company Name]
Income Statement
For the Eight Months Ending [Date]

Gross Sales   _____

Cost of Goods Sold:
    Beginning Inventory   _____
    Materials   _____
    Labor and Subcontractors   _____

    Less: Ending Inventory   _____
    Cost of Goods Sold   _____

Gross Profit   _____

General Expenses:
    Salaries and Wages   _____
    Payroll Taxes   _____
    Rent   _____
    Utilities   _____
    Telephone   _____
    Office   _____
    Automotive and Truck   _____
    Depreciation   _____
    Dues and Subscriptions   _____
    Operating Supplies   _____
    Repairs and Maintenance   _____
    Equipment Rental   _____
    Insurance   _____
    Interest   _____
    Legal and Accounting   _____
    Total General Expenses   _____

Net Profit   _____

[Your Company Name]
Statement of Cash Flows
For the Eight Months Ending [Date]

Sources of Funds:

        Net profits from operations   _____

        Plus non-cash expenses:

            Depreciation   _____

        Loan proceeds   _____

        From sale of capital assets   _____

        Total Sources of Funds   _____

Applications of Funds:

        Loan principal payments   _____

        Purchase of capital assets   _____

        Draw for living expenses   _____

        Reduction in Long-term Liabilities   _____

        Total Applications of Funds   _____

Increase in Funds   _____

Changes in Working Capital:	Beginning	End	Change
Cash	_____	_____	_____
Accounts Receivable	_____	_____	_____
Inventory	_____	_____	_____
Accounts Payable	_____	_____	_____
Current Notes Payable	_____	_____	_____
Taxes Payable	_____	_____	_____
Total Changes	_____	_____	_____

Goals and Assumptions Worksheets

Goal # _____

_____

_____

_____

Assumptions:

_____

_____

_____

_____

_____

Steps	Due date	Completed

How to Use the Disk

Inside the back cover of this book you'll find a compact disk with 14 blank forms. These include checklists, analysis and evaluation forms, budget and expense templates, and worksheets. To use these forms, you'll need a computer running Windows 95 or later.

Each of the 14 forms comes in two computer formats, Microsoft Word and Acrobat® Reader. If you have Microsoft Word 97 or later installed on your computer, that's the best choice. Install only the forms for Word. If you don't have a recent version of Microsoft Word, install the forms in Acrobat® Reader format. These 14 forms are almost as useful in Acrobat® Reader as they are in Word. The advantage in using Microsoft Word is that you can modify a form to meet your needs and then save the changed form to disk. You can fill in the blanks on Acrobat® Reader forms, but you can't save the changes to disk.

No matter which set of forms you install, less than 1 Mb of hard drive space is required.

To use the 14 forms in Acrobat® Reader format, you'll need the Acrobat® Reader program. If you don't already have Acrobat® Reader, program installation is one of the options on the disk. Acrobat® Reader will use about 6 Mb on your hard drive.

How to Install the Forms

Insert the disk in your CD-ROM drive. After a few seconds, the light on the front of your CD-ROM drive should come on and the green installation screen should appear. If installation doesn't begin automatically, click on the My Computer icon on your desktop. Navigate to your CD drive. The disk name is Land_development. Double click on the file Demo32.exe. You'll see the following options on a green background:

* Install Word Forms
* Install Acrobat® Reader Forms
* Install Acrobat® Reader
* View Links
* Exit

Select the type of form you want to install from the installation screen.

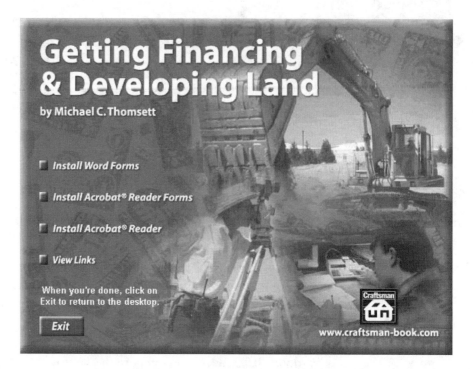

Click on the option of your choice and follow the instructions on the screen. When installation is complete, you'll be returned to the green screen, Getting Financing & Developing Land. When you've installed all the forms you need, click on Exit.

Like most modern installation programs, the CD in the back of this book uses the Microsoft Installer. If this is the first time you've installed using the Microsoft Installer, you'll have to reboot your computer to complete the process. Follow instructions on the screen.

The installation process puts a new Financing Forms icon on your desktop. Clicking on that icon should open a window with a list of all forms installed. Double-clicking on the form name should open the form of your choice. If a form doesn't open, it's because you don't have the correct program installed, either Microsoft Word or Acrobat® Reader. Install Acrobat® Reader and then try double-clicking once again on the form name.

Word Forms

Word forms are document (.doc) files you can fill out and print in Microsoft Word or many other word processing programs. It's easy to change the formatting on these files. Maybe *too* easy. We recommend that you type in your own company name or insert a company logo on the form. Then save each form under a new name. That way you'll always have the original available if you want to start again from scratch. If you corrupt a form on your hard disk, you can always reload from the CD. But be aware that reloading resets all forms to their original condition. That will wipe out changes if you saved to disk without changing the file name.

If you want to reload a single form, use Windows Explorer to copy from the CD onto the Financing Forms directory.

Acrobat® Reader Forms

Acrobat® Reader forms are Portable Document Format (.PDF) files you can fill out and print in Adobe's Acrobat® Reader. You can fill in most blanks and type words or numbers anywhere you see brackets: [ ]. There's no way to save the form as it was changed, so each time you use one of these PDF files you'll have to add your company information again. But Acrobat® Reader does produce professional-looking documents that you won't corrupt by accident. If you don't already have Adobe's Acrobat® Reader, it's one of the options on the installation screen.

Here's something to remember about PDF files. Words and numbers you type on the form don't really exist as part of the document until you tab or click, *out* of that cell. So don't print the form until the insertion cursor is out of the last cell you filled in.

View Links

This option on the installation screen offers links to several Web pages which may be useful to you, including an amortization calculator. The calculator figures what your payments will be for any loan, any term, at any interest rate. If you have a dial-up connection to the Internet, you may have to connect before these links will work.

You can also go directly to the calculator without using the CD. Just type the following on the address line of your browser and press Enter:

http://costbook.com/cbcstore/prodpages/info/gfd/amort_calc.htm

Index

Practical References for Builders

Basic Lumber Engineering for Builders

Beam and lumber requirements for many jobs aren't always clear, especially with changing building codes and lumber products. Most of the time you rely on your own "rules of thumb" when figuring spans or lumber engineering. This book can help you fill the gap between what you can find in the building code span tables and what you need to pay a certified engineer to do. With its large, clear illustrations and examples, this book shows you how to figure stresses for pre-engineered wood or wood structural members, how to calculate loads, and how to design your own girders, joists and beams. Included FREE with the book — an easy-to-use version of NorthBridge Software's *Wood Beam Sizing* program. **272 pages, 8¹/₂ x 11, $38.00**

Contractor's Guide to QuickBooks Pro 2005

This user-friendly manual walks you through QuickBooks Pro's detailed setup procedure and explains step-by-step how to create a first-rate accounting system. You'll learn in days, rather than weeks, how to use *QuickBooks Pro* to get your contracting business organized, with simple, fast accounting procedures. On the CD included with the book you'll find a *QuickBooks Pro* file preconfigured for a construction company (you drag it over onto your computer and plug in your own company's data). You'll also get a complete estimating program, including a database, and a job costing program that lets you export your estimates to *QuickBooks Pro*. It even includes many useful construction forms to use in your business. **344 pages, 8¹/₂ x 11, $49.75**
Also available: **Contractor's Guide to QuickBooks Pro 2001, $45.25**
Contractor's Guide to QuickBooks Pro 2003, $47.75
Contractor's Guide to QuickBooks Pro 2004, $48.50

National Concrete & Masonry Estimator

Since you don't get every concrete or masonry job you bid, why generate a detailed list of materials for each one? The data in this book will allow you to get a quick and accurate bid, and allow you to do a detailed material takeoff, only for the jobs you are the successful bidder on. Includes assembly prices for bricks, and labor and material prices for brick bonds, brick specialties, concrete blocks, CMU, concrete footings and foundations, concrete on grade, concrete specialties, concrete beams and columns, beams for elevated slabs, elevated slab costs, and more. Includes a CD-ROM with an electronic version of the book with *National Estimator*, a stand-alone *Windows*™ estimating program, plus an interactive multimedia video that shows you how to use the disk to compile construction cost estimates. **672 pages, 8¹/₂ x 11, $54.00. Revised annually**

Estimating with Microsoft *Excel*

Most builders estimate with *Excel* because it's easy to learn, quick to use, and can be customized to your style of estimating. Here you'll find step-by-step how to create your own customized automated spreadsheet estimating program for use with *Excel*. You'll learn how to use the magic of *Excel* in creating detail sheets, cost breakdown summaries, and linking. You can even create your own macros. Includes a CD-ROM that illustrates examples in the book and provides you with templates you can use to set up your own estimating system. **148 pages, 8¹/₂ x 11, $39.95**

National Repair & Remodeling Estimator

The complete pricing guide for dwelling reconstruction costs. Reliable, specific data you can apply on every repair and remodeling job. Up-to-date material costs and labor figures based on thousands of jobs across the country. Provides recommended crew sizes; average production rates; exact material, equipment, and labor costs; a total unit cost and a total price including overhead and profit. Separate listings for high- and low-volume builders, so prices shown are specific for any size business. Estimating tips specific to repair and remodeling work to make your bids complete, realistic, and profitable. Includes a CD-ROM with an electronic version of the book with *National Estimator*, a stand-alone *Windows*™ estimating program, plus an interactive multimedia video that shows you how to use the disk to compile construction cost estimates. **312 pages, 8¹/₂ x 11, $53.50. Revised annually**

Estimating & Bidding for Builders & Remodelers

This 4th edition has all the information you need for estimating and bidding new construction and home improvement projects. It shows how to select jobs that will be profitable, do a labor and materials take-off from the plans, calculate overhead and figure your markup, and schedule the work. Includes a CD with an easy-to-use construction estimating program and a database of 50,000 current labor and material cost estimates for new construction and home improvement work, with area modifiers for every zip code. Price updates on the Web are free and automatic. **272 pages, 8¹/₂ x 11, $69.50**

Estimating Home Building Costs

Estimate every phase of residential construction from site costs to the profit margin you include in your bid. Shows how to keep track of manhours and make accurate labor cost estimates for footings, foundations, framing and sheathing finishes, electrical, plumbing, and more. Provides and explains sample cost estimate worksheets with complete instructions for each job phase. **320 pages, 5¹/₂ x 8¹/₂, $17.00**

National Construction Estimator

Current building costs for residential, commercial, and industrial construction. Estimated prices for every common building material. Provides manhours, recommended crew, and gives the labor cost for installation. Includes a CD-ROM with an electronic version of the book with *National Estimator*, a stand-alone *Windows*™ estimating program, plus an interactive multimedia video that shows how to use the disk to compile construction cost estimates. **664 pages, 8¹/₂ x 11, $52.50. Revised annually**

Construction Forms & Contracts

125 forms you can copy and use — or load into your computer (from the FREE disk enclosed). Then you can customize the forms to fit your company, fill them out, and print. Loads into Word for *Windows*™, *Lotus 1-2-3*, *WordPerfect*, *Works*, or *Excel* programs. You'll find forms covering accounting, estimating, fieldwork, contracts, and general office. Each form comes with complete instructions on when to use it and how to fill it out. These forms were designed, tested and used by contractors, and will help keep your business organized, profitable and out of legal, accounting and collection troubles. Includes a CD-ROM for *Windows*™ and Macintosh. **400 pages, 8¹/₂ x 11, $41.75**

Contractor's Guide to the Building Code Revised

This new edition was written in collaboration with the International Conference of Building Officials, writers of the code. It explains in plain English exactly what the latest edition of the *Uniform Building Code* requires. Based on the 1997 code, it explains the changes and what they mean for the builder. Also covers the *Uniform Mechanical Code* and the *Uniform Plumbing Code*. Shows how to design and construct residential and light commercial buildings that'll pass inspection the first time. Suggests how to work with an inspector to minimize construction costs, what common building shortcuts are likely to be cited, and where exceptions may be granted. **320 pages, 8¹/₂ x 11, $39.00**

CD Estimator

If your computer has *Windows*™ and a CD-ROM drive, *CD Estimator* puts at your fingertips 85,000 construction costs for new construction, remodeling, renovation & insurance repair, electrical, plumbing, HVAC and painting. You'll also have the *National Estimator* program — a stand-alone estimating program for *Windows*™ that *Remodeling* magazine called a "computer wiz." Quarterly cost updates are available at no charge on the Internet. To help you create professional-looking estimates, the disk includes over 40 construction estimating and bidding forms in a format that's perfect for nearly any word processing or spreadsheet program for *Windows*™. And to top it off, a 70-minute interactive video teaches you how to use this CD-ROM to estimate construction costs. **CD Estimator is $78.50**

Markup & Profit: A Contractor's Guide

In order to succeed in a construction business, you have to be able to price your jobs to cover all labor, material and overhead expenses, and make a decent profit. The problem is knowing what markup to use. You don't want to lose jobs because you charge too much, and you don't want to work for free because you've charged too little. If you know how to calculate markup, you can apply it to your job costs to find the right sales price for your work. This book gives you tried and tested formulas, with step-by-step instructions and easy-to-follow examples, so you can easily figure the markup that's right for your business. Includes a CD-ROM with forms and checklists for your use. **320 pages, 8¹/2 x 11, $32.50**

Land Development

The industry's bible. Nine chapters cover everything you need to know about land development from initial market studies to site selection and analysis. New and innovative design ideas for streets, houses, and neighborhoods are included. Whether you're developing a whole neighborhood or just one site, you shouldn't be without this essential reference. **360 pages, 5¹/2 x 8¹/2, $55.00**

National Renovation & Insurance Repair Estimator

Current prices in dollars and cents for hard-to-find items needed on most insurance, repair, remodeling, and renovation jobs. All price items include labor, material, and equipment breakouts, plus special charts that tell you exactly how these costs are calculated. Includes a CD-ROM with an electronic version of the book with *National Estimator*, a stand-alone *Windows*™ estimating program, plus an interactive multimedia video that shows how to use the disk to compile construction cost estimates. **576 pages, 8¹/2 x 11, $54.50. Revised annually**

Rough Framing Carpentry

If you'd like to make good money working outdoors as a framer, this is the book for you. Here you'll find shortcuts to laying out studs; speed cutting blocks, trimmers and plates by eye; quickly building and blocking rake walls; installing ceiling backing, ceiling joists, and truss joists; cutting and assembling hip trusses and California fills; arches and drop ceilings — all with production line procedures that save you time and help you make more money. Over 100 on-the-job photos of how to do it right and what can go wrong. **304 pages, 8¹/2 x 11, $26.50**

Building Contractor's Exam Preparation Guide

Passing today's contractor's exams can be a major task. This book shows you how to study, how questions are likely to be worded, and the kinds of choices usually given for answers. Includes sample questions from actual state, county, and city examinations, plus a sample exam to practice on. This book isn't a substitute for the study material that your testing board recommends, but it will help prepare you for the types of questions — and their correct answers — that are likely to appear on the actual exam. Knowing how to answer these questions, as well as what to expect from the exam, can greatly increase your chances of passing. **320 pages, 8¹/2 x 11, $35.00**

The Contractor's Legal Kit

Stop "eating" the costs of bad designs, hidden conditions, and job surprises. Set ground rules that assign those costs to the rightful party ahead of time. And it's all in plain English, not "legalese." For less than the cost of an hour with a lawyer you'll learn the exclusions to put in your agreements, why your insurance company may pay for your legal defense, how to avoid liability for injuries to your sub and his employees or damages they cause, how to collect on lawsuits you win, and much more. It also includes a FREE computer disk with contracts and forms you can customize for your own use. **352 pages, 8¹/2 x 11, $69.95**

Contracting in All 50 States

Every state has its own licensing requirements that you must meet to do business there. These are usually written exams, financial requirements, and letters of reference. This book shows how to get a building, mechanical or specialty contractor's license, qualify for DOT work, and register as an out-of-state corporation, for every state in the U.S. It lists addresses, phone numbers, application fees, requirements, where an exam is required, what's covered on the exam and how much weight each area of construction is given on the exam. You'll find just about everything you need to know in order to apply for your out-of-state license. **416 pages, 8¹/2 x 11, $36.00**

How to Succeed With Your Own Construction Business

Everything you need to start your own construction business: setting up the paperwork, finding the work, advertising, using contracts, dealing with lenders, estimating, scheduling, finding and keeping good employees, keeping the books, and coping with success. If you're considering starting your own construction business, all the knowledge, tips, and blank forms you need are here. **336 pages, 8¹/2 x 11, $28.50**